Literacy skills through Rhyme and Rhythm

For the Multi-Ability Classroom

Noelle Cahill and Marion Pratt

OXFORD UNIVERSITY PRESS AUSTRALIA

Oxford New York
Athens Auckland Bangkok Bombay
Calcutta Cape Town Dar es Salaam Delhi
Florence Hong Kong Istanbul Karachi
Kuala Lumpur Madras Madrid Melbourne
Mexico City Nairobi Paris Port Moresby
Singapore Taipei Tokyo Toronto

and associated companies in
Berlin Ibadan

OXFORD is a trade mark of Oxford University Press

© Noelle Cahill, Marion Pratt 1996
First published 1996
Reprinted 1996

This book is copyright. Apart from any fair dealing for
the purposes of private study, research, criticism or review
as permitted under the Copyright Act, no part may be
reproduced, stored in a retrieval system, or transmitted,
in any form or by any means, electronic, mechanical,
photocopying, recording, or otherwise without prior
written permission. Enquiries to be made to Oxford
University Press.

Copying for educational purposes
Where copies of part or the whole of the book are
made under Part VB of the Copyright Act, the law requires that
prescribed procedures be followed.
For information, contact the Copyright Agency Limited.

National Library of Australia
Cataloguing-in-Publication data:

Cahill, Noelle.
    Literacy skills through rhyme and rhythm: for the
    multi-ability classroom.
    Bibliography.
    ISBN 0 19 553757 2.

    1.Poetry – Study and teaching (Primary). 2. Language arts
    (Primary). I. Pratt, Marion, 1940 – . II. Title. (Series :
    Classroom connections).

372.64

Edited by Ronel Redman
Text design by Tim Kotsiakos
Cover design by Kirstin Lowe
Cover and text illustrations by Nathan Jurevicius
Typeset by Sandra Sheehan
Printed through Bookpac Production Services, Singapore
Published by Oxford University Press,
253 Normanby Road, South Melbourne, Australia

Contents

Acknowledgments	iv
Introduction	1
Scope and Skills Chart	2
Instructional Model	4
Oral Stage	5
Early Written Stage	6
Advanced Written Stage	7
Before You Begin	8
Additional Resources	9
Lesson Outlines:	
• *Jeremiah Obadiah*	10
• *Anger, Anger, Anger*	16
• *A Swamp Romp*	22
• *Wriggles and Giggles*	28
• *I Know Something*	34
• *Little Arabella Miller*	40
• *The Kangaroo*	46
• *The Parcel*	52
• *As I Was*	58
• *Junk*	64
• *If You Should Meet a Crocodile*	70
• *Brenda Baker*	76
• *Ode to an Extinct Dinosaur*	82
• *The Teacher Took My Tennis Ball*	88
• *Car Attack*	94
• *Storm Came*	100
Look What I Can Do	106
Poems I Like	107
My Favourite Poem	108

Acknowledgments

Our thanks to Geoff Pratt for his valuable consultancy assistance and for his contribution in the editing and managing of the manuscript.

Our thanks also to Virginia Lowe for making available her personal collection of poetry for children, to Chris Gilligan and Freya Green for their practical classroom advice and to Brian Cahill for his support.

The authors and publisher wish to thank the following copyright holders for granting permission to reproduce poems:

Libby Hathorn, C/-Curtis Brown (Aust.) P/L, Sydney for 'Junk', 'A Teacher Took My Tennis Ball' and 'Storm Came' by Libby Hathorn, from *Talks with my Skateboard*;

Penguin Books Australia Ltd for 'Swamp Romp', 'Brenda Baker', 'Ode to an Extinct Dinosaur', 'Car Attack' by Doug MacLeod, from *In The Garden of Bad Things*.

Disclaimer

Every effort has been made to trace the original source of material used in this book. Where the attempt has been unsuccessful, the authors and publisher would be pleased to hear from the copyright holders in order to rectify any errors or omissions.

Introduction

This book is a response to the cries of many teachers with whom we have worked over the years.

'How can I reach all the children in my class?

'The range is too great. I have gifted children and children with learning difficulties.'

'What about the students who work without demanding the extra attention they deserve?'

As professionals, teachers give their best but some children are never reached. So often, after the classroom has emptied, teachers are haunted by small faces, eyes focused somewhere in the middle distance, restless hands plaiting and replaiting the hair of the child in front of them; teachers know too well the superficial signs of boredom, apathy and lack of understanding.

One answer to this age-old problem, we found, lay in the seductive power of rhyme. Teaching literacy skills through the rhyme and rhythm of poetry has been practised successfully for many years in a variety of schools. This method allows the less able child to feel secure working within the framework of a known poem, graded activities make provision for the able learner and open-ended activities stimulate the talented student. This ensures effective acquisition of literacy skills in the multi-ability classroom combined with learning enjoyment.

Literacy Skills Through Rhyme and Rhythm is designed to teach literacy skills through the medium of poetry to children from Prep level through to Year 4. The carefully selected poems, together with their accompanying skills, are divided into two stages:

- **Oral stage**: The activities within this stage familiarise the children with the poem through enjoyable physically-based activities. Learning the poem by rote establishes the rhyming pattern as a base for proceeding from the known to the unknown. Carefully graded oral questions and discussion topics ensure that all levels of thinking can be challenged.
- **Written stage**: Activities for each poem are pitched at Base, Middle and Advanced skill levels. Depending on the composition of the class the teacher is free to choose all, or only one or two of the levels. The less able child may work within the framework of a known poem; graded activities stimulate and challenge the more able learner; open-ended activities stimulate the talented child.

Reproducible activity sheets are located after the Written stage of each poem. Personal record sheets are provided at the back of the book to record individual efforts outside of the formal lesson and satisfy the 'I've got nothing to do!' cries (see page 8).

Work through these poems with the children.

Teach more literacy skills using poetry.

Pass on the delight and power of words.

Noelle Cahill and Marion Pratt

Scope and Skills Chart

YEAR LEVEL	POEM TITLE	SKILLS	REPRODUCIBLE SKILLS SHEETS	LINKS
Years Prep–1	Jeremiah Obadiah Anonymous	Initial sounds Rhyming words	1 Poem — Initial sounds 2 Initial sound 3 Cloze exercise	Physical activities
Years Prep–1	Anger, Anger, Anger Marion Pratt	Word recognition Initial sounds	1 Poem — Initial sound 'a' 2 Jigsaw — Word recognition 3 Broken words — Initial sounds	Emotions
Years 1–2	A Swamp Romp Doug MacLeod	Initial blends Onomatopoeia (Sound words)	1 Jungle scene — Initial blends 2 Sound words 3 Wordsearch grid	Tactile experiences
Years 1–2	Wriggles and Giggles Anonymous	Double letters Action words	1 Grid — Double letters 2 Poem — Double letter words 3 Frame sheet — Action words	Differences
Years 1–2	I Know Something Anonymous	Spelling Silent letters 'k' and 'w'	1 Poem — Spelling 2 Spelling 3 Silent letters 'k' and 'w'	Secrets
Years 1–2	Little Arabella Miller Anonymous	Double consonants Quotation marks	1 Poem — Double consonants 2 Double consonants 3 Quotation marks	Creatures
Years 1–2	The Kangaroo Anonymous	Blends Spelling long 'i' words	1 Blends 'mp' 2 Kangaroo — Long 'i' words 3 Long 'i' words	Australian animals
Years 1–2–3	The Parcel Marion Pratt	Sentence structure Spelling 'ou' and 'ow' words	1 Sentence structure 1 2 Sentence structure 2 3 Spelling 'ou' and 'ow'	Postage/Birthdays

YEAR LEVEL	POEM TITLE	SKILLS	REPRODUCIBLE SKILLS SHEETS	LINKS
Years 1–2–3	As I Was Anonymous	Alphabetical ordering Spelling 'ay' and 'a-e'	1 Poem — Alphabetical ordering 2 Street sheet — 'ay' words 3 'ay' and 'a-e'	The absurd
Years 2–3	Junk Libby Hathorn	Action words — Present/Past tense Onomatopoeia (Sound words)	1 Action words 2 Sound words 3 Present/Past tense	Technology

Years 2–3	If You Should Meet a Crocodile
	Anonymous
		Commands
		Spelling 'i-e' words
			1 Poem — Spelling 'i-e' words
			  — Commands
			2 Crocodile shape — 'i-e' words
			  — Commands
			3 Maze 'i-e' words
				Reptiles big and small

Years 2–3	Brenda Baker Doug MacLeod	Antonyms (Opposites) Alliteration (Bo bit Bill)	1 Sea scene — Antonyms 2 Antonyms 3 Alliteration	Sea creatures
Years 2–3	Ode to an Extinct Dinosaur Doug MacLeod	Synonyms Internal double consonants	1 Synonym jigsaw 2 Synonyms 3 Internal double consonants	Prehistoric animals
Years 2–3–4	The Teacher Took My Tennis Ball Libby Hathorn	Contractions Quotation marks	1 Contractions 1 2 Contractions 2 3 Quotation marks	Discipline
Years 2–3–4	Car Attack Doug MacLeod	Rhyming words Compound words	1 Compound words 1 2 Compound words 2 3 Crossword	Unusual people
Years 2–3–4	Storm Came Libby Hathorn	Word extension Metaphors	1 Extended words wordsearch 2 Extended words 3 Extended words verse sheet	'Feeling' the weather

Instructional model

1 Children **MEMORISE** the poem

2 Whole class **ORAL** activities

3 Ability groups **WRITTEN** activities

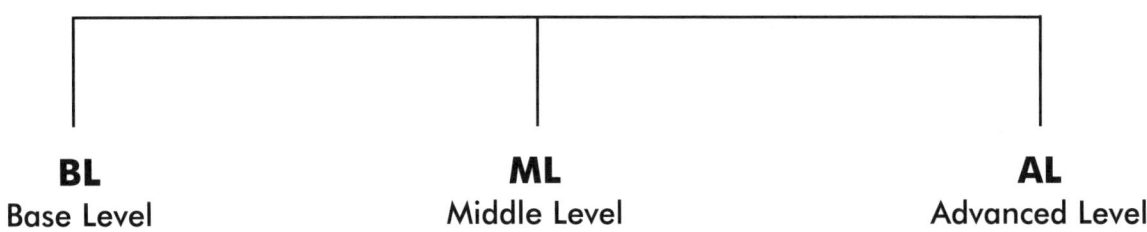

BL
Base Level

ML
Middle Level

AL
Advanced Level

1 It is essential that children MEMORISE the poem through oral activities before progressing to the written stage. This strategy ensures:
  - progression from the known to the unknown
  - confidence with language
  - opportunity for mature readers to manipulate and experiment with new formats
  - facility for less mature readers to 'read' the poem at the visual stage.
2 ORAL ACTIVITIES involve the whole class. Children participate at their own level of ability. The graded questions provided allow teachers to target children appropriately.
3 WRITTEN ACTIVITIES require that an **enlarged copy of the poem** is always on display. These activities are provided at three levels. The teacher determines the appropriate use of levels according to the children's needs.

Oral Stage

The oral stage of each poem develops the auditory skills of rhyme, performance, word awareness, memory training and levels of thinking.

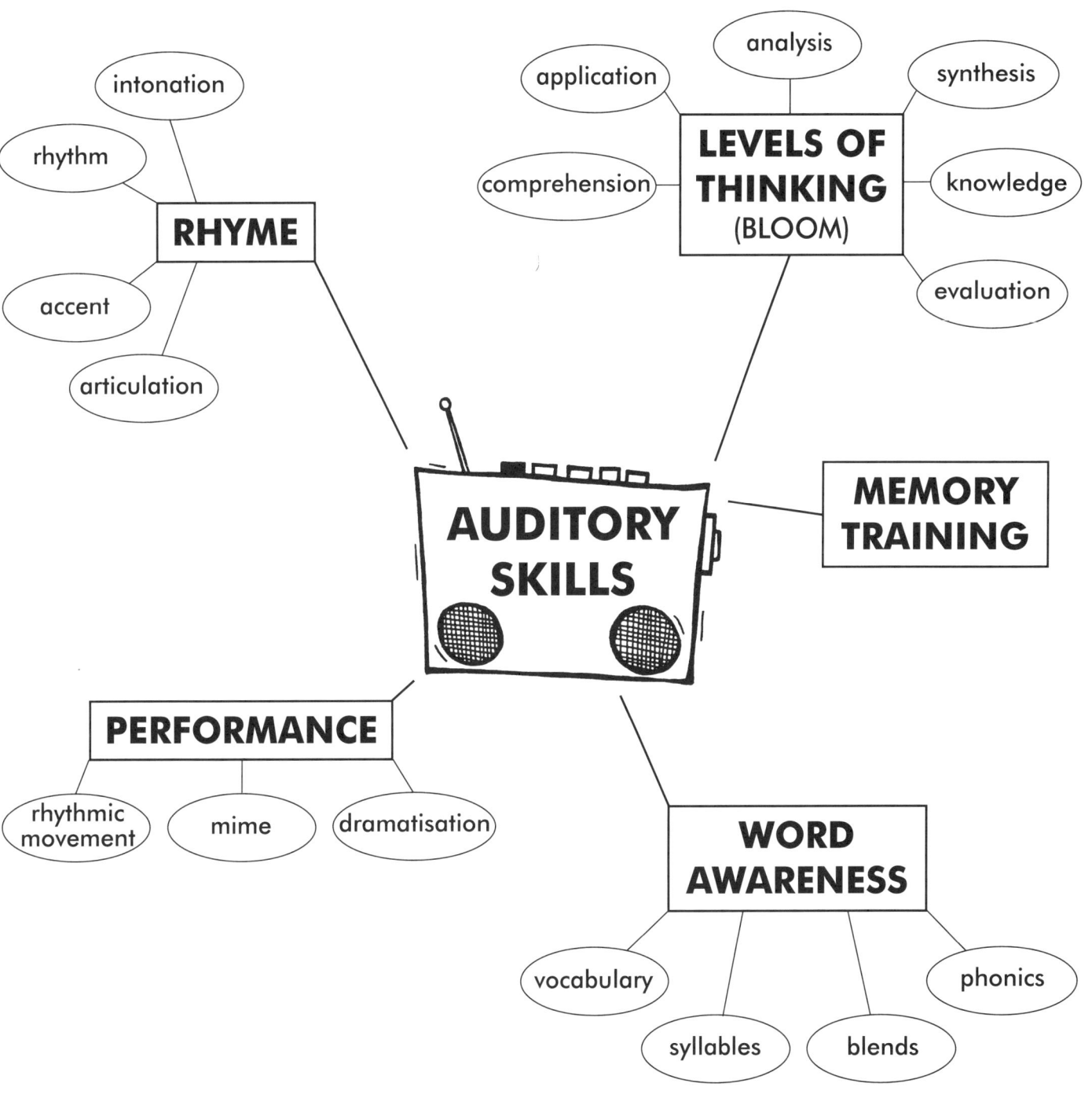

Early Written Stage

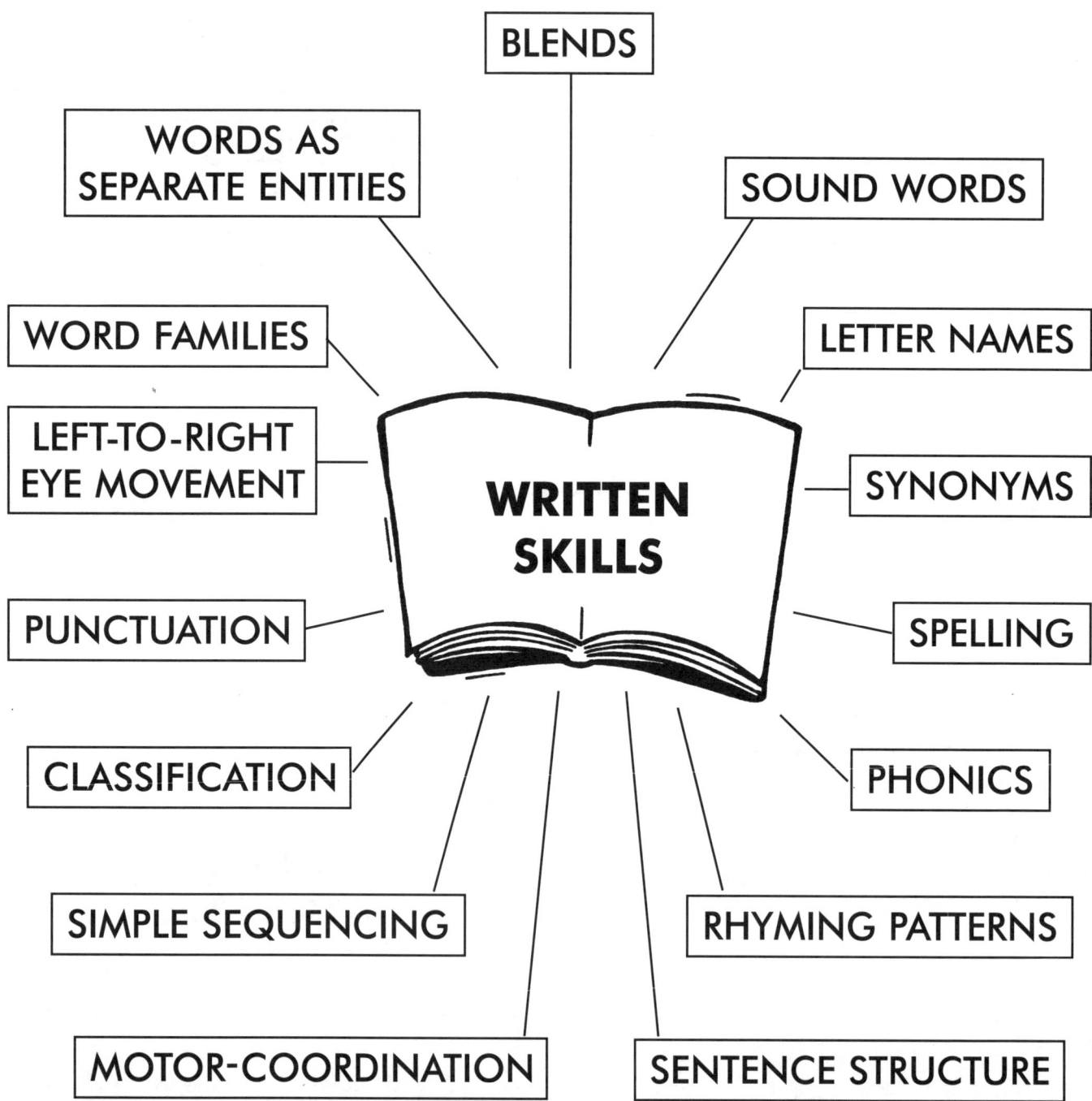

Advanced Written Stage

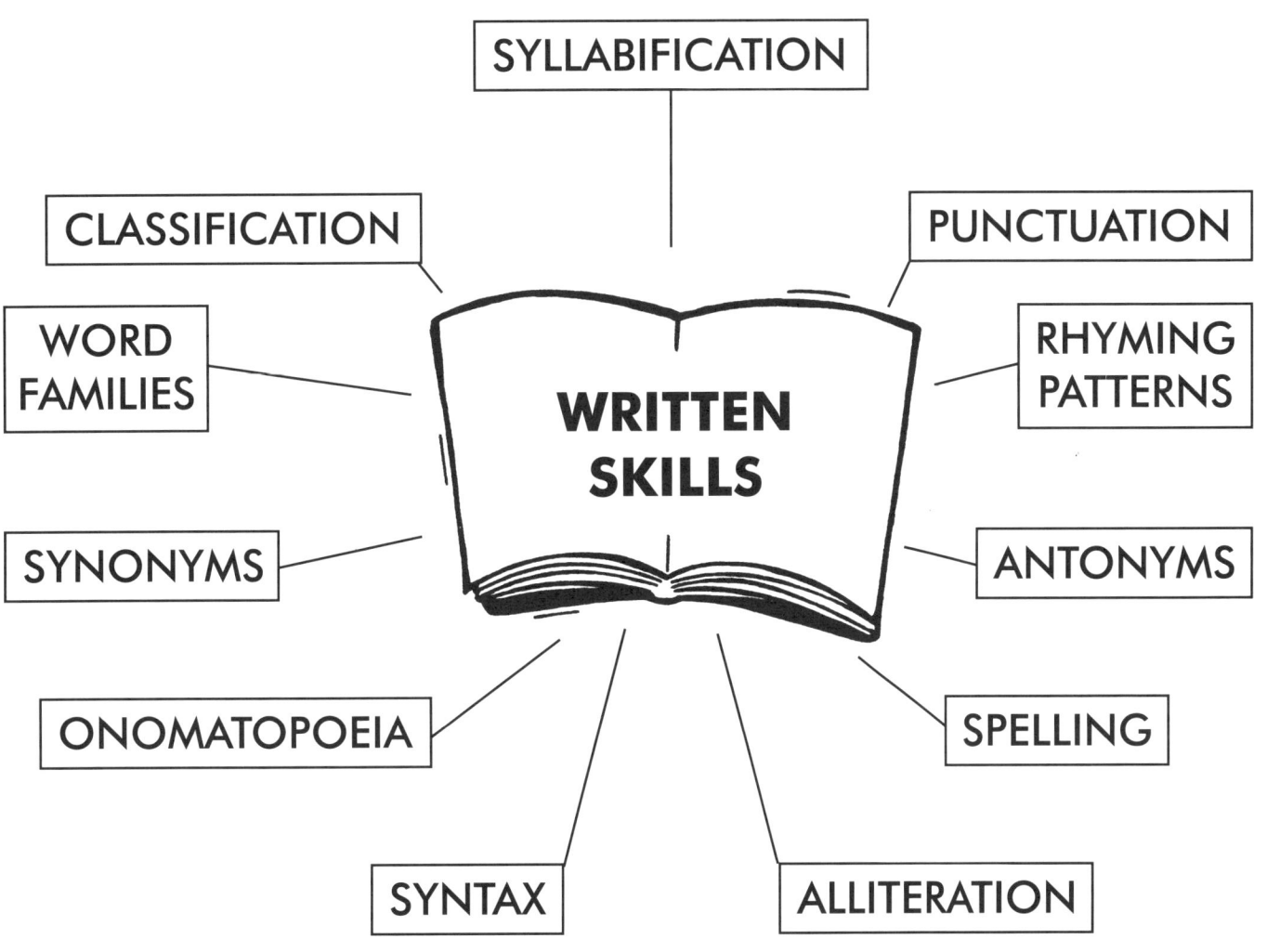

Before You Begin

REMEMBER

Always have a large copy of the poem on display.

'Look What I Can Do' Record Sheet

Encourage children to record dates of activities done with class exercises, and then to create and record their own activities from individually chosen poems.

Use:

- after each class
- with further poems chosen by the child
- ten minutes to spare?

Introduce any new terms

e.g. shape poem, metaphor, alliteration.

'Poems I Like' Record Sheet

Encourage children to browse and collect titles and authors of favourite poems. Record these.

'My Favourite Poem' Record Sheet

Have a poetry month. Collect poems from other children, parents, grandparents, teachers. Read them together. Create a poster wall of favourite poems using these sheets.

Additional Resources

Coats, Lucy   *First Rhymes*, Orchard Books, 1994
Forster, John (comp.)   *Twinkle Twinkle Chocolate Bar*, Oxford University Press, 1991
Hathorn, Libby   *Talks With My Skateboard*, ABC Corporation, 1981
MacLeod, Doug   *In the Garden of Badthings*, Kestrel Books, 1981
Prelutsky, Jack (selected)   *For Laughing Out Loud*, Red Fox Books, Random House, 1991
Prelutsky, Jack (selected)   *The Walker Book of Poetry*, Walker Books, 1985
Rosen, Michael (selected)   *Poems for the Very Young*, R.D. Press, N.S.W., 1993
Schafer, Diane & Cheryl Irving (comp.)   *Celery Noise and Quiet Cheese*, Oxford University Press, 1988

Note: Look for rhythm, length, particular interests, effective word use, specific literacy skills and overall appeal.

JEREMIAH OBADIAH

Jeremiah Obadiah
　　puff, puff, puff.

When he races up the hill he
　　huffs, huffs, huffs.

When he goes to school by day he
　　roars, roars, roars.

When he goes to bed at night he
　　snores, snores, snores.

When he has a funny dream he
　　snuffs, snuffs, snuffs.

Jeremiah Obadiah
　　puff, puff, puff.

Anonymous

Skills:	Initial sounds
	Rhyming words
Skill sheets:	Poem—Initial sounds
	Initial sounds
	Cloze exercise
Link to:	Physical activities

- Walk, jump, run 20 metres. Listen to other children's heart beats. Note huffs and puffs.
- Investigate reasons for differences.
- Make a big book. Follow the pattern of Jeremiah, substituting story book characters, activities and actions.

 JEREMIAH OBADIAH

ORAL STAGE

- Recite the poem to the class.
- Recite the poem again, this time drawing attention to the rhythm.

  On the main beat the children pound their clenched fist into the palm of the other hand.

- Recite the poem, stopping after the first word of each second line.

  The children complete each second line.

- Divide the class into two groups.

  Group 1 recites the poem with the teacher. Group 2 performs the actions. Reverse group roles and repeat.

 ## Discussion: Sounds people make.

- Recite the poem together with the class.
- Ask questions at appropriate levels:
  1. What does Jeremiah do when he goes to school?
  2. Where is Jeremiah when he 'snores, snores, snores'?
  3. Do you think Jeremiah is a quick person or a slow person?
  4. What sounds do you make when you race up a hill?
  5. Would you like Jeremiah if he were your brother? Why/Why not?
  6. What might his funny dream have been about?
- Children recite the poem as they march on the spot. They take turns to perform Jeremiah's actions.

JEREMIAH OBADIAH

WRITTEN STAGE

Visual presentation: Teacher/child uses a pointer and recites the poem, substituting or omitting words and/or consonants. Nominate a child to isolate and correct words.

Base Level

- Hand out a copy of the poem to each child (page 13).

  The children write over words as directed by the teacher, e.g.: Three words beginning with 'p'. A word beginning with 'w'.

- Copy and distribute the Initial Sound sheet (page 14).

  The children cut out each letter, then cut into the marked sections. Ask them to remake each letter and paste the pieces onto a blank page. They could colour the letter before cutting to help them identify the pieces.

Middle Level

- Copy and distribute the Cloze Exercise sheet (page 15).

  Ask the children to find and fill in the missing words.

- Hand out a 6-page blank booklet to each child.

  The children write and illustrate each part of the poem on a page to make up their own book.

  The children make a comic strip of Jeremiah's activities.

Advanced Level

- Distribute chart paper to the children.

  Following the same pattern as 'Jeremiah Obadiah', the children write a poem about someone else.

  Children present their poems in the form of a wall chart.

  Each child rewrites 'Jeremiah Obadiah', replacing some words with different rhyming words. They swap their poem with a group member and correct.

Name: _____

JEREMIAH OBADIAH
Reproducible Skill Sheet 1— **Initial sounds**

Jeremiah Obadiah
  puff, puff, puff.
When he races up the hill he
  huffs, huffs, huffs.
When he goes to school by day he
  roars, roars, roars.
When he goes to bed at night he
  snores, snores, snores.
When he has a funny dream he
  snuffs, snuffs, snuffs.
Jeremiah Obadiah
  puff, puff, puff.

JEREMIAH OBADIAH
Reproducible Skill Sheet 2 — **Initial sounds**

1. Cut out each letter.
2. Cut through all the marked pieces.
3. Remake each letter.
4. Paste the letter pieces onto a blank page.

Name: _____

JEREMIAH OBADIAH
Reproducible Skill Sheet 3 — Cloze exercise

Fill in the missing words and letters.

Jeremiah Obadiah
p _ _ _ , p _ _ _ , p _ _ _ .
When he races up the _ _ _ _ he huffs, _ _ _ _ _ , _ _ _ _ _ .
_ _ _ _ he goes to _ _ _ _ _ _ by day he roars, _ _ _ _ _ , _ _ _ _ _ .
When he _ _ _ _ to bed at _ _ _ _ _ he
_ _ _ _ _ _ , _ _ _ _ _ _ , _ _ _ _ _ _ .
When _ _ has a _ _ _ _ _ dream he
_ _ _ _ _ _ , _ _ _ _ _ _ , _ _ _ _ _ _ .
Jeremiah Obadiah
p _ _ _ , _ _ _ _ , _ _ _ _ .

©N.Cahill & M.Pratt, *Literacy Skills Through Rhyme and Rhythm*, Oxford University Press, 1996.

15

ANGER, ANGER, ANGER

Anger, anger, anger.
Slump in a chair and pull your hair.

Anger, anger, anger.
Jump up and down and frown and frown.

Anger, anger, anger.
Go red in the face and start to pace.

Then shake your body,
And start to smile.

You'll feel better
In a little while.

I hope.

Marion Pratt

Skills: Word recognition
Initial sounds

Skill sheets: Poem—Initial sound 'a'
Rhyming words
Jigsaw—Word recognition
Broken words—Initial sounds

Link to: Emotions
- Brainstorm different emotions.
- Make masks from large circles depicting a range of emotions.
- Mime simple scenes highlighting an emotion. Use masks. Children guess emotion.

ANGER, ANGER, ANGER

ORAL STAGE

- Recite the poem to the class.
- Recite the poem again, this time with appropriate actions.

  The children join in, reciting the first line of the first 3 couplets. They then join in further as familiarity increases.

- Encourage the children to dramatise the poem.

Discussion: Anger—reasons, types, methods of expression.

- Recite the poem together with the class.
- Ask questions at appropriate levels:
  1. When do you feel angry?
  2. What do you do?
  3. When does Mum or Dad slump? Why?
  4. Why do you shout or scream?
  5. Tell how someone made you angry. How did you react?
  6. What might have been a better way?

- Recite the poem to the class with deletions, e.g. 'Anger, anger, anger./Slump in a _____.'

  Children say the missing word(s).

- Recite the poem to the class, introducing mistakes, e.g. 'Anger, anger, anger./Bump in a chair …'

  Children name the incorrect consonant/blend.

- Introduce the 'match the rhyming pattern' activity, e.g.: The teacher chooses two children and says the initial word 'face' and taps one child's shoulder to start. The pattern continues— 'lace', 'hace', 'mace', 'race', 'gace' — until one child falters or repeats a word.

ANGER, ANGER, ANGER

WRITTEN STAGE

Visual presentation: Teacher/child uses a pointer and recites the poem, substituting or omitting words and/or consonants. Nominate a child to isolate and correct words.

Base Level

- Hand out a copy of the poem to each child (page 19).

  The children write over all the 'A's, and 'a's.

  Ask children to draw an angry face. Surround the face with 'a's.

- Copy and distribute the Anger jigsaw sheet (page 20).

  The children cut out all the pieces and paste the pieces in correct order.

Middle Level

- Hand out a copy of the poem to each child (page 19).

  Say a word from the poem and ask the children to write over the word. Continue until most words are written over.

  Children collect all the rhyming words from the poem. They make a list and add more.

- Copy and distribute the Broken Word sheet (page 21).

  The children cut out the single letters and paste them into the frames to remake words from the poem.

Advanced Level

- Children write thesaurus lists for 'pull', 'jump', 'pace', 'little'.
- Children research expressions of anger in animals and humans and report to the class.
- Children create their own 'Anger' poem.

ANGER, ANGER, ANGER
Reproducible Skill Sheet 1— **Initial sounds**

Name: _____

Anger, anger, anger.
Slump in a chair and pull your hair.
Anger, anger, anger.
Jump up and down and frown and frown.
Anger, anger, anger.
Go red in the face and start to pace.
Then shake your body,
And start to smile.
You'll feel better
In a little while.
I hope.

ANGER, ANGER, ANGER
Reproducible Skill Sheet 2 — Recognition jigsaw

> Anger, anger, anger.
> Slump in a chair and pull your hair.
>
> Anger, anger, anger.
> Jump up and down and frown and frown.

1 Cut out the jigsaw pieces.
2 Arrange the words in their correct order to match the lines from the poem.
3 Paste the pieces onto a blank page.

Anger,	Slump	in	a	pull	anger,	hair.
chair	anger.	and	your			
Jump	down	Anger,	up	frown	and	
and	frown.	and	anger,	anger.		

©N.Cahill & M.Pratt, *Literacy Skills Through Rhyme and Rhythm*, Oxford University Press, 1996.

ANGER, ANGER ANGER
Reproducible Skill Sheet 3 — **Initial sounds**

Name: _____

1 Cut out the single letters at the bottom of the page.
2 Paste each letter into a frame to make a word from the poem.

nger	etter
rown	air
lump	ull

a   h   p
s   f   b

©N.Cahill & M.Pratt, *Literacy Skills Through Rhyme and Rhythm*, Oxford University Press, 1996.

A SWAMP ROMP

Clomp Thump
Swamp Lump
Plodding in the Ooze,
Belly Shiver
Jelly Quiver
Squelching in my Shoes.

Clomp Thump
Romp Jump
Mulching in the Mud,
Boot Trudge
Foot Sludge
Thud! Thud! Thud!

Doug MacLeod

Skills: Initial blends
Onomatopoeia (sound words)

Skill sheets: Jungle scene—Initial blends
Sound words
Wordsearch grid

Link to: Tactile experiences
- Draw large footwear for varying weather conditions. Write captions on footwear. Cut out and paste around room. (e.g. sandals slop, boots trudge)
- Make a collage of a swamp scene.
- Collect objects of different textures. Place one in a bag. Children feel and name. Repeat.

A SWAMP ROMP

ORAL STAGE

- Recite the poem to the class, using appropriate voice and movements.
- Recite the poem as above, with the children arranged in a circle.

  The children trudge in a clockwise direction.
- Repeat the poem to the class, deleting the last word of each line.

  The children complete each line and jump to the last three words of the poem.
- Divide the class into two groups.

  Recite the poem together with the class. Group 1 plods to the beat and Group 2 squelches (drag their feet) to the beat.

Discussion: Sensory experiences:
Tactile (touch)
Kinaesthetic (feel)

- Recite the poem together with the class.
- Ask questions at appropriate levels:
  1. What shivered?
  2. What did he squelch in?
  3. Where did he plod?
  4. What else oozes?
  5. What would his parents think?
  6. Where do you think he was?
- Divide the class into two groups.

  Group 1 says the poem with enthusiasm; Group 2 chants 'plod plod plod' to the main beat.

A SWAMP ROMP

WRITTEN STAGE

Visual presentation: Teacher/child uses a pointer and recites the poem, substituting or omitting words and/or consonants. Nominate a child to isolate and correct words.

Base Level

- Copy and distribute the Jungle Scene sheet (page 25).

  Ask the children to fill the blanks by writing in the correct blends.

  The children cut out the blends, paste these on a blank page and complete each word.

  They illustrate each word.

Middle Level

- Copy and distribute the Sound Words sheet (page 26).

  The children complete the words from the list.

  They illustrate each word with a sound picture.

  Work in groups to create a swamp scene. Reproduce blend words from the poem onto the scene.

Advanced Level

- Copy and distribute the Wordsearch grid (page 27).

  Individually or in pairs children design a wordsearch using words from the poem. Share the result with the class.

  Children write a poem using the 6-line pattern of 'A Swamp Romp'.

  Each child draws an imaginary swamp scene and adds sound words in appropriate places.

A SWAMP ROMP
Reproducible Skill Sheet 1— **Initial blends**

Name: _____

A Jungle Scene

1. Write the blends below in the gaps to make a jungle word.
2. Cut out each blend, paste them on a blank page and complete the word. Illustrate each word.

_ _ ump

_ _ udge

_ _ omp

_ _ od

_ _ amp

_ _ udge

| cl | sw | sl | th | tr | pl |

©N.Cahill & M.Pratt, *Literacy Skills Through Rhyme and Rhythm*, Oxford University Press, 1996.

A SWAMP ROMP
Reproducible Skill Sheet 2 — Sound words

Name: _____

1 Complete the words. Use the list to help you.
2 Illustrate each word with a sound picture.

| clomp |
| thump |
| plod |
| shiver |
| squelch |
| trudge |
| thud |
| quiver |

_ h u _

_ l o _ p

p _ _ _

s h _ v _ _

th _ _ p

_ _ u e _ c h

q _ i v _ _

_ r u _ g e

26 ©N.Cahill & M.Pratt, *Literacy Skills Through Rhyme and Rhythm*, Oxford University Press, 1996.

Name: _____

A Swamp Romp Wordsearch

Make up your own wordsearch using words from the poem.

WRIGGLES AND GIGGLES

Polly, Solly, Katy, Billy,

All are fun but very silly.

   Polly prattles.

   Solly wriggles.

   Katy rattles.

   Billy giggles.

Have you ever heard such rattling,

Wriggling, giggling, noise and prattling?

Anonymous

Skills: Double letters
Action words

Skill sheets: Grid—Double letters
Poem—Double letter words
Frame sheet—Action words

Link to: Differences
- Talk about situations and reactions, e.g. First day at school; New baby in the family. Note different reactions. Talk about why.
- Interview teachers, the principal, the secretary on their first day at school. Make posters.

Ms Flap felt _____ when _____

WRIGGLES AND GIGGLES

ORAL STAGE

- Recite the poem to the class.
- Repeat the poem to the class.

  Ask the children to slap both hands on their knees to the beat (Polly = 1st beat). They clap their hands to the second beat (Solly = 2nd beat). Continue the slap/clap pattern to the main beat of the poem.

- Recite the poem to the class again.

  The children continue the above actions, joining in the last word of each line.

- Recite the poem together with the class.

  Four children dramatise the roles of Polly, Solly, Katy and Billy.

- Divide the class into two groups.

  Group 1 says lines 1, 2, 7 and 8. Group 2 says lines 3, 4, 5 and 6.

Discussion: Why do people giggle, wriggle, rattle or prattle?

- Recite the poem together with the class.
- Ask questions at appropriate levels:
  1. Who are the two boys?
  2. Who are the two girls?
  3. What does Billy do?
  4. What kind of children are they?
  5. Can you imagine some other actions?
  6. Where would you expect to see children behaving like Polly, Solly, Katy and Billy?
- Recite the poem to the class with accompanying slap/clap actions.

  Nominate four children to face the group as Polly, Solly, Katy and Billy. Each child bobs down the first time his/her name is said. Each child stands up the second time his/her name is said.

WRIGGLES AND GIGGLES

WRITTEN STAGE

Visual presentation: Teacher/child uses a pointer and recites the poem, substituting or omitting words and/or consonants. Nominate a child to isolate and correct words.

Base Level

- Copy and distribute the Double Letters grid (page 31).

  Ask the children to colour in all the double letter groups in the grid.

- Hand out a copy of the poem to each child (page 32).

  The children write over all the double letter words in the poem.

- Copy and distribute the Frame sheet (page 33).

  The children write each character's name from the poem beneath a frame and draw the character in the frame.

Middle Level

- Copy and distribute the Double Letters grid (page 31).

  The children colour in all the double letter groups in the grid.

  Children cut out all the double letter groups from the grid and paste them on a blank page. Leave space at **each side** of the double letters. Then, add letters to make words.

- Copy and distribute the Frame sheet (page 33).

  The children write each character's name and action from the poem beneath a frame. Then they illustrate the character in action (e.g. Polly prattles).

Advanced Level

- Hand out a blank page to each child.

  Each child constructs a blank grid with a minimum of 10 x 10 squares. They write double letter words from the poem on their grid and fill remaining blanks with random letters.

  Children list alternative action words which describe the poem characters' behaviour.

- Copy and distribute the Frame sheet (page 33).

  The children draw the poem characters and their actions in the frames. Then they write the name and action beneath each frame.

Name: _____

WRIGGLES AND GIGGLES
Reproducible Skill Sheet 1— Double letters

Colour in all the double letter groups.

t	t	e	r	g	g	m	n
m	l	l	o	f	f	d	i
n	n	s	g	g	a	t	t
i	g	g	c	y	d	o	k
r	t	t	s	g	t	l	l
g	g	e	s	s	o	n	r

©N.Cahill & M.Pratt, *Literacy Skills Through Rhyme and Rhythm*, Oxford University Press, 1996.

WRIGGLES AND GIGGLES
Reproducible Skill Sheet 2 — Double letter words

Name: _____

Write over all the double letter words in the poem.

Polly, Solly, Katy, Billy,
All are fun but very silly.
  Polly prattles.
  Solly wriggles.
  Katy rattles.
  Billy giggles.
Have you ever heard such rattling,
Wriggling, giggling, noise and prattling?

Name: _____

WRIGGLES AND GIGGLES
Reproducible Skill Sheet 3 — Action words

Picture frames

1 Draw a picture of each character in the poem.
2 Write their name and action word beneath their picture.

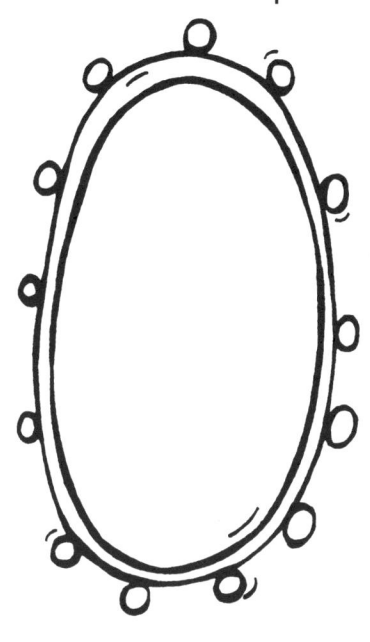

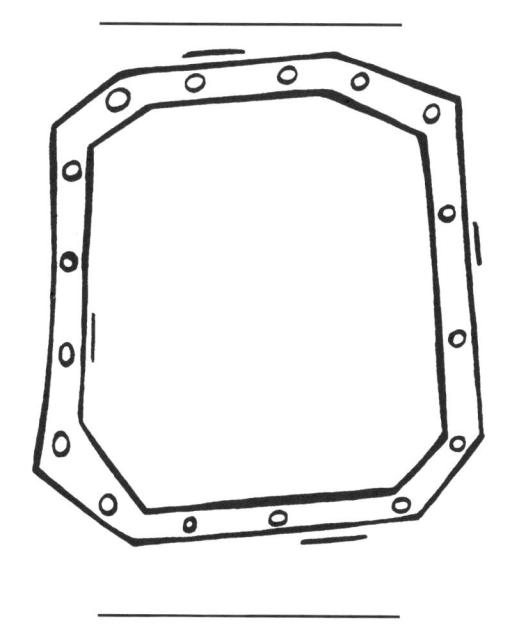

©N.Cahill & M.Pratt, *Literacy Skills Through Rhyme and Rhythm*, Oxford University Press, 1996.

I KNOW SOMETHING

I know something I won't tell.

Three cheeky monkeys in a peanut shell.

One can read and one can write

And one can shout with all his might.

Anonymous

Skills: Spelling
Silent letters 'k', 'w'

Skill sheets: Poem—Spelling
Spelling
Silent letters 'k', 'w'

Link to: Secrets
- Discuss when to keep secrets and when to tell.
- Write imaginary secrets starting with the first line of the poem. Post in a box. Read just before lunch (no names).

I KNOW SOMETHING

ORAL STAGE

- Recite the poem to the class.
- Recite the poem again, emphasising the rhythm.

  Ask the children to pat their thighs to the beat.
- Recite the poem to the class, stopping before the last word of each line.

  The children say the last word of each line.

Discussion: Do you know something you won't tell? Why?

- Recite the poem together with the class, tramping on the spot.
- Ask questions at appropriate levels:
  1. How many monkeys were there?
  2. Where were the three cheeky monkeys?
  3. What did the monkey do 'with all his might'?
  4. What can you do with all your might?
  5. Can you imagine some other things the monkeys might do?
  6. How do you feel when people won't tell you something?
- Organise the children to stand and face a partner.

  The children whisper the poem in secretive voices to each other.

I KNOW SOMETHING

WRITTEN STAGE

Visual presentation: Teacher/child uses a pointer and recites the poem, substituting or omitting words and/or consonants. Nominate a child to isolate and correct words.

Base Level

- Hand out a copy of the poem to each child (page 37).
- Randomly select some words from the poem and say them to the class.

  As the teacher says each word the children circle it.

  Children then write over each circled word.

- Each child makes a booklet with one line of the poem per page. They illustrate each page.

Middle Level

- Copy and distribute the Spelling Skill sheet (page 38).

  Ask the children to read the poem on the sheet and to circle words which do not belong to the original poem.

  The children list the correct words in order. Then add more rhyming words alongside, following the same pattern. Have a partner test their spelling.

- Copy and distribute the Silent Letter sheet (page 39).

  Children look at the picture and write the matching word in the circle by following the diagonal line.

Advanced Level

- Make available a collection of classroom books and dictionaries.

  The children use classroom books to find words beginning with a silent 'k' and silent 'w'. Make up a class list.

  Using the list, they arrange and write these silent letter words in dictionary order.

  They exchange their list with a partner and test each other's spelling skills.

Name: _____

I KNOW SOMETHING
Reproducible Skill Sheet 1— **Spelling**

I know something I won't tell.
Three cheeky monkeys in a peanut shell.
One can read and one can write
And one can shout with all his might.

©N.Cahill & M.Pratt, *Literacy Skills Through Rhyme and Rhythm*, Oxford University Press, 1996.

I KNOW SOMETHING
Reproducible Skill Sheet 2 — Spelling

Name: _____

1. Circle the words which do not belong to the poem.
2. Write the correct word in the left column.
3. Write matching rhyming words in the right column.
4. Watch your spelling!

> I low something I don't fell.
> Tree cheeky monkeys in a peanut well.
> One fan read and one man write
> And one van shout with all his light.

Correct Word	Rhyming Words

I KNOW SOMETHING
Reproducible Skill Sheet 3 — silent letters 'K' and 'W'

Name: _____

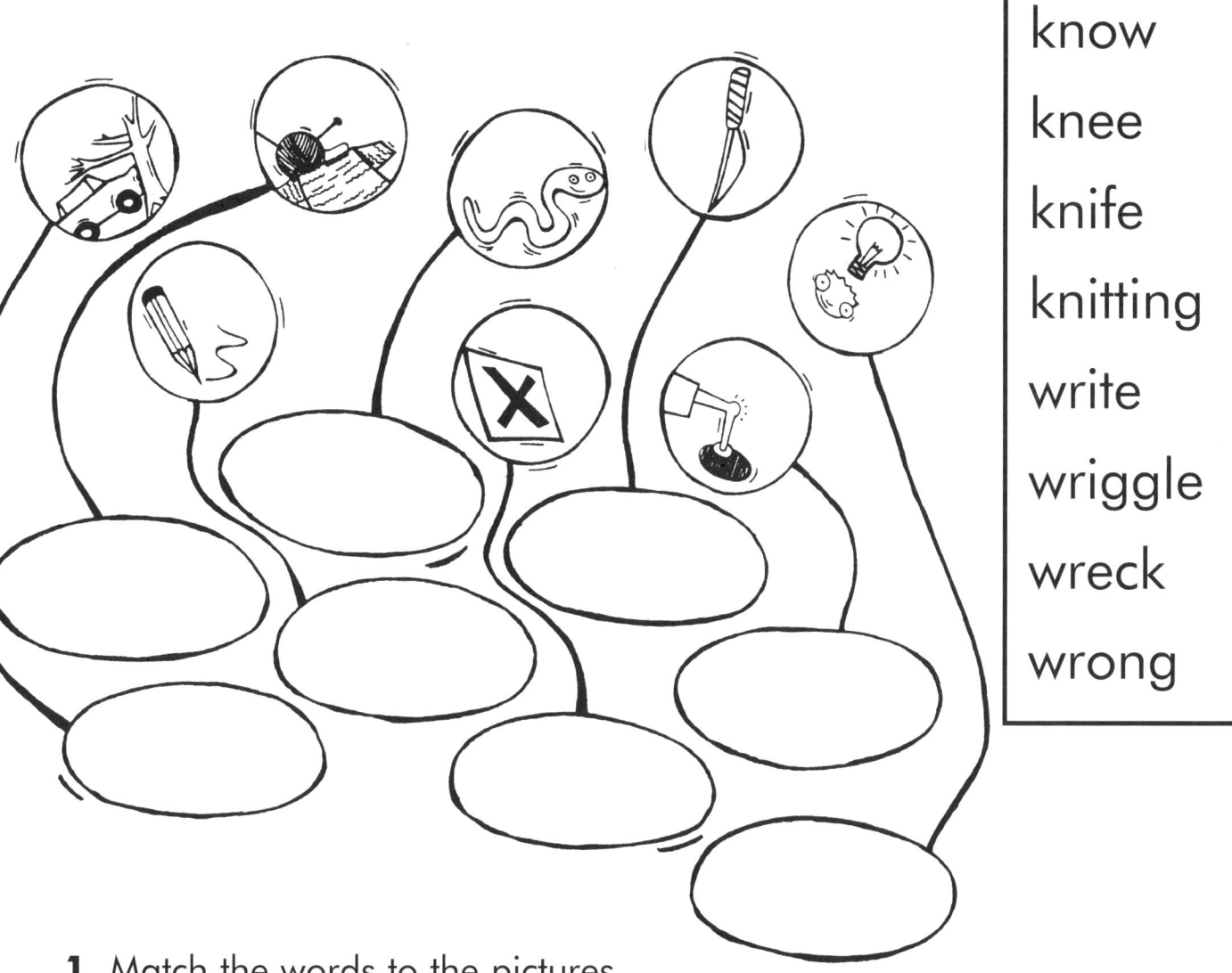

| know |
| knee |
| knife |
| knitting |
| write |
| wriggle |
| wreck |
| wrong |

1 Match the words to the pictures.
2 Follow the line from the picture. Write the matching word in the circle.
3 Turn the sheet over. Write each word in a sentence.

©N.Cahill & M.Pratt, *Literacy Skills Through Rhyme and Rhythm*, Oxford University Press, 1996.

LITTLE ARABELLA MILLER

Little Arabella Miller
Found a woolly caterpillar.
First it crawled upon her mother,
Then upon her baby brother.
All said, 'Arabella Miller,
Take away that caterpillar.'

Anonymous

Skills: Double consonants
Quotation marks

Skill sheets: Poem—Double consonants
Double consonants—cut and paste
Quotation marks

Link to: Creatures
- Brainstorm for names of creatures.
- Cut out a very long creature shape and attach it to the classroom walls. Fill it with names and illustrations of creatures.

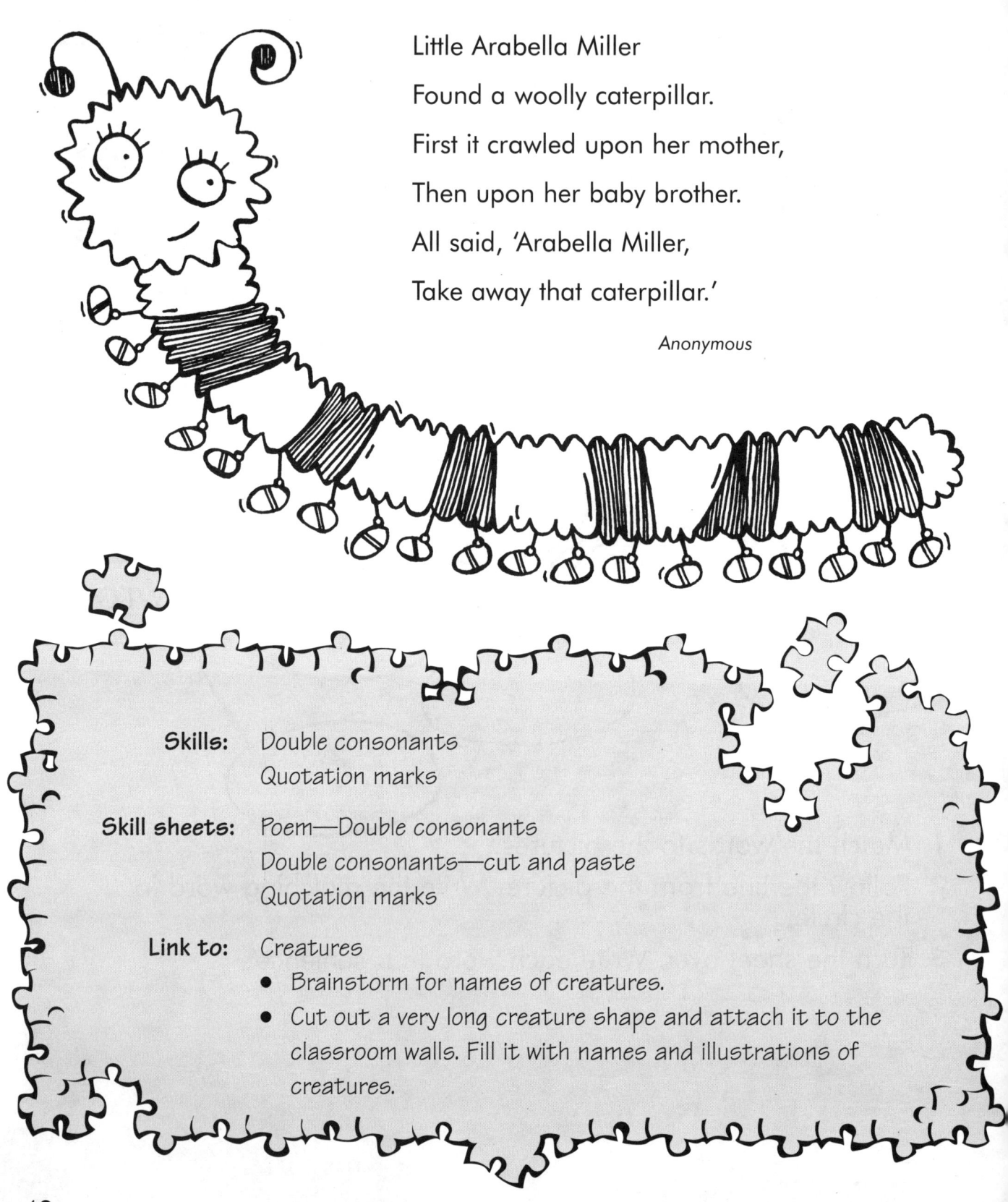

LITTLE ARABELLA MILLER

ORAL STAGE

- Recite the poem to the class, clapping the four main beats in each line.

  Ask the children to join in and clap the four-beat pattern.

- Recite the poem to the class or nominate a child to recite. Stop at 'All said,'.

  In turns or together, the children complete the poem with expressions, e.g. surprise, fear, revulsion.

Discussion: Creepy Crawly Creatures

- Recite the poem together with the class.

- Ask questions at appropriate levels:

  1 What did Arabella find?
  2 Who did it crawl over?
  3 What would you say if a caterpillar crawled on you?
  4 How many woolly things can you think of?
  5 What do you think Arabella will do with the caterpillar?
  6 If you were the caterpillar, what would you say?

- Recite the first two words of each line to the class. The children complete the line, e.g.
  Teacher: 'Little Arabella'
  Children: 'Miller'
  Teacher: 'Found a'
  Children: 'woolly caterpillar'.

- Recite the poem silently to the class.

  The children watch the teacher's lips. The teacher stops at different places and a nominated child says the next word.

- Divide the class into two groups (Group A and Group B).

  The whole class recites the poem. On lines 1, 3 and 5, Group A bobs down.
  On lines 2, 4 and 6, Group B bobs down.

LITTLE ARABELLA MILLER

WRITTEN STAGE

Visual presentation: Teacher/child uses a pointer and recites the poem, substituting or omitting words and/or consonants. Nominate a child to isolate and correct words.

Base Level

- Hand out a copy of the poem to each child (page 43).

  Ask the children to circle all the double letters.

  Ask the children to draw a long caterpillar and fill it up with different double letters.

- Copy and distribute the Double Consonants sheet (page 44) and strips of coloured paper.

  The children cut and paste paper over the double letter outlines. Ask them to find more double letter words.

Middle Level

- With the class, make a list of words with double consonants.

  The children write sentences in which they include words from the list.

- Each child makes up a 6-page booklet with the lines from the poem. Illustrate each page.

- Ask the children to make up a story in which a caterpillar crawled on four people they know.

  They draw the people and write what each one would say. Follow this pattern: Kate said, "_____."

Advanced Level

- Copy and distribute the Quotation sheet (page 45).

  The children write a story about an imaginary creature. Include at least three quotations from the skill sheet.

  Children create a code (e.g. A = 1, B = 2). They write a message in code to an imaginary creature using several double letter words. Send the message to a classmate to decipher.

  The children make up a crossword using only double letter words. Swap with a partner to complete the crossword.

LITTLE ARABELLA MILLER
Reproducible Skill Sheet 1— **Double consonants**

Name: _____

Little Arabella Miller
Found a woolly caterpillar.
First it crawled upon her mother,
Then upon her baby brother.
All said, 'Arabella Miller,
Take away that caterpillar.'

LITTLE ARABELLA MILLER
Reproducible Skill Sheet 2 — **Double consonants**

Name: _____

1 Cut out some coloured paper.
2 Paste the paper to fill each letter shape.

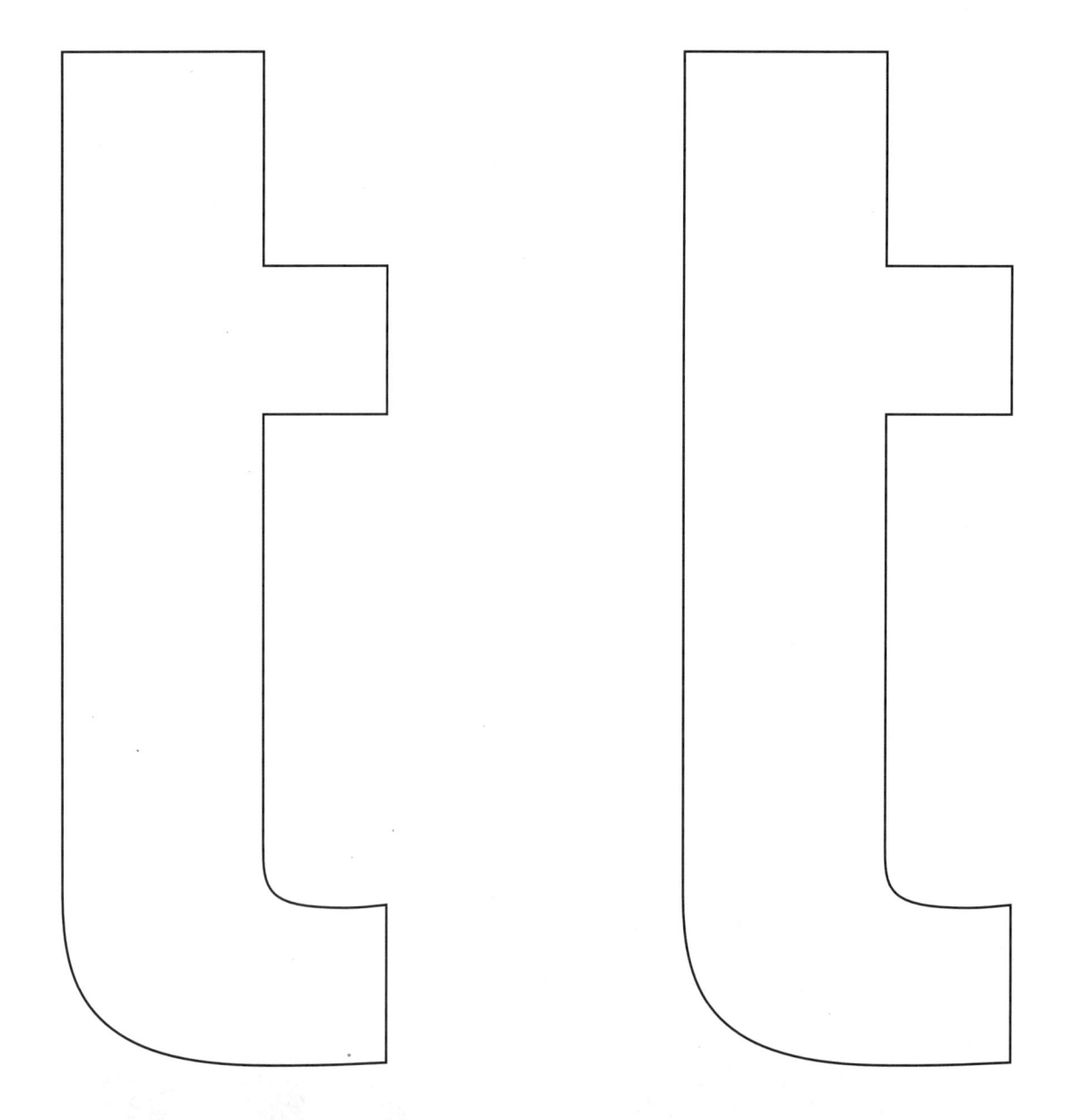

LITTLE ARABELLA MILLER
Reproducible Skill Sheet 3 — **Quotation marks**

Name: _____

1 Write a story about an imaginary creature.
2 Include some of these quotations in your story. Don't forget the quotation marks.

"It's squirming and writhing"

"Get out of my hair"

"I need a friend."

"Ugh"

"What a delicious little person"

©N.Cahill & M.Pratt, *Literacy Skills Through Rhyme and Rhythm*, Oxford University Press, 1996.

THE KANGAROO

Old Jumpety-Bumpety-Hop-and-Go-One
Was lying asleep on his side in the sun.
This old kangaroo, he was whisking the flies
With his long glossy tail from his ears and his eyes.
Jumpety-Bumpety-Hop-and-Go-One
Was lying asleep on his side in the sun,
Jumpety-Bumpety-Hop.

Anonymous

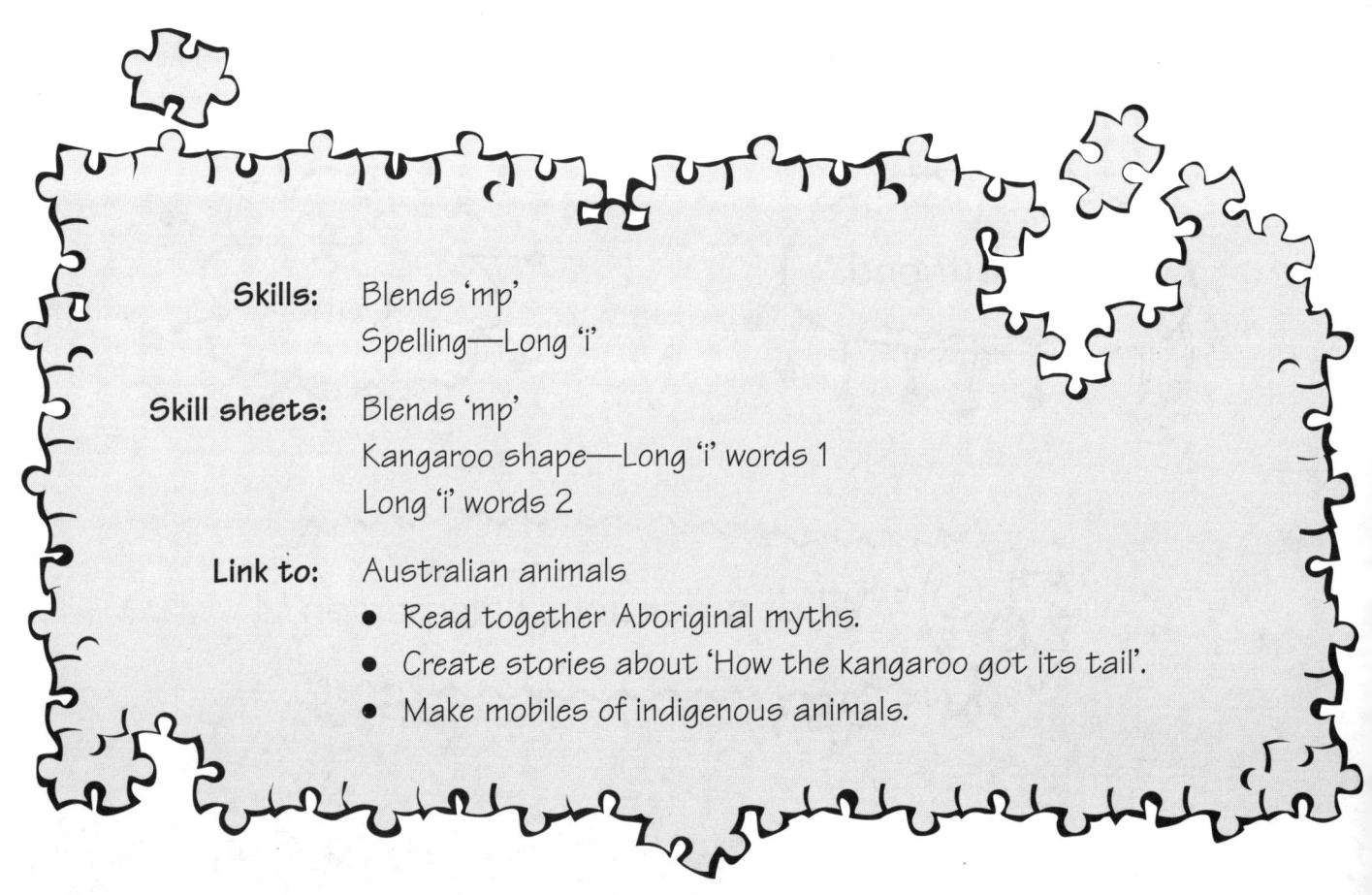

Skills: Blends 'mp'
Spelling—Long 'i'

Skill sheets: Blends 'mp'
Kangaroo shape—Long 'i' words 1
Long 'i' words 2

Link to: Australian animals
- Read together Aboriginal myths.
- Create stories about 'How the kangaroo got its tail'.
- Make mobiles of indigenous animals.

THE KANGAROO

ORAL STAGE

- Recite the poem to the class.
- Recite the poem to the class again.

  Invite the children to stamp to the beat.

- Recite the poem together with the class.

  Nominate children to hop to the lines containing 'Jumpety-Bumpety-Hop'.

Discussion: Animal movements.

- Recite the poem together with the class.
- Ask questions at appropriate levels:

  1 What was the kangaroo whisking from his ears and eyes?
  2 What was the kangaroo's name?
  3 Is it day-time or night-time?
  4 Why was he whisking the flies?
  5 What other things can be whisked away?
  6 In what ways do older animals usually behave?

- Arrange the class into seven groups. Each group represents a line of the poem.

  Point to each group in turn. The groups chant the lines in order.

  Point to groups randomly, working through the poem line by line. Groups recite their new line.

THE KANGAROO

WRITTEN STAGE

Visual presentation: Teacher/child uses a pointer and recites the poem, substituting or omitting words and/or consonants. Nominate a child to isolate and correct words.

Base Level

- Copy and distribute the Blends sheet (page 49).

    Ask the children to write over all the 'mp' blends and then to illustrate the words.

    Children rewrite the first two lines of the poem, changing the last word of each line to maintain the rhyming pattern.

- Copy and distribute the Kangaroo sheet (page 50).

    Children write their favourite words from the poem around the kangaroo. Include long 'i' words.

Middle Level

- Copy and distribute the Long 'i' Word sheet (page 51).

    The children find and list all the long 'i' words in the poem.

    Children study the list of words and sort all the long 'i' words into families.

    Ask the children to use some long 'i' words in rhyming couplets.

Advanced Level

- Make available classroom books for children to use.

    The children make a comprehensive list of long 'i' sounding words. Use books in the room as a resource.

    Children refer to the list and write a story, including most of the long 'i' words.

    Children write rhyming couplets about different animals. They dramatise these for the class.

THE KANGAROO
Reproducible Skill Sheet 1— **Blends 'mp'**

Name: _____

1 Write over the 'mp' blends.
2 Draw a picture alongside each word.

stump

limp

bump

thump

trumpet

hump

crumpet

lamp

©N.Cahill & M.Pratt, *Literacy Skills Through Rhyme and Rhythm*, Oxford University Press, 1996.

49

THE KANGAROO
Reproducible Skill Sheet 2 — Long 'i' words

Name: _____

1. Write your favourite words from the poem around the kangaroo.
2. Include some long 'i' words.

THE KANGAROO
Reproducible Skill Sheet 3 — **Long 'i' words**

Name: _____

1 Make a list of all the long 'i' words in the poem.

2 Put them in groups.

i	**ie**	**y**	**i–e**
kind	tries	cry	pile

3 Turn the page over and write some rhymes. Here are two examples.

I wonder why
I sometimes cry

Three little mice
Ate heaps of rice

©N.Cahill & M.Pratt, *Literacy Skills Through Rhyme and Rhythm*, Oxford University Press, 1996.

THE PARCEL

I walked to the letter-box
And what did I see?
A big brown parcel just for me.
I shook it.
I poked it.
I yelled, "Yippee!"

Whisper what you think I found
In that parcel,
Tightly bound.

Marion Pratt

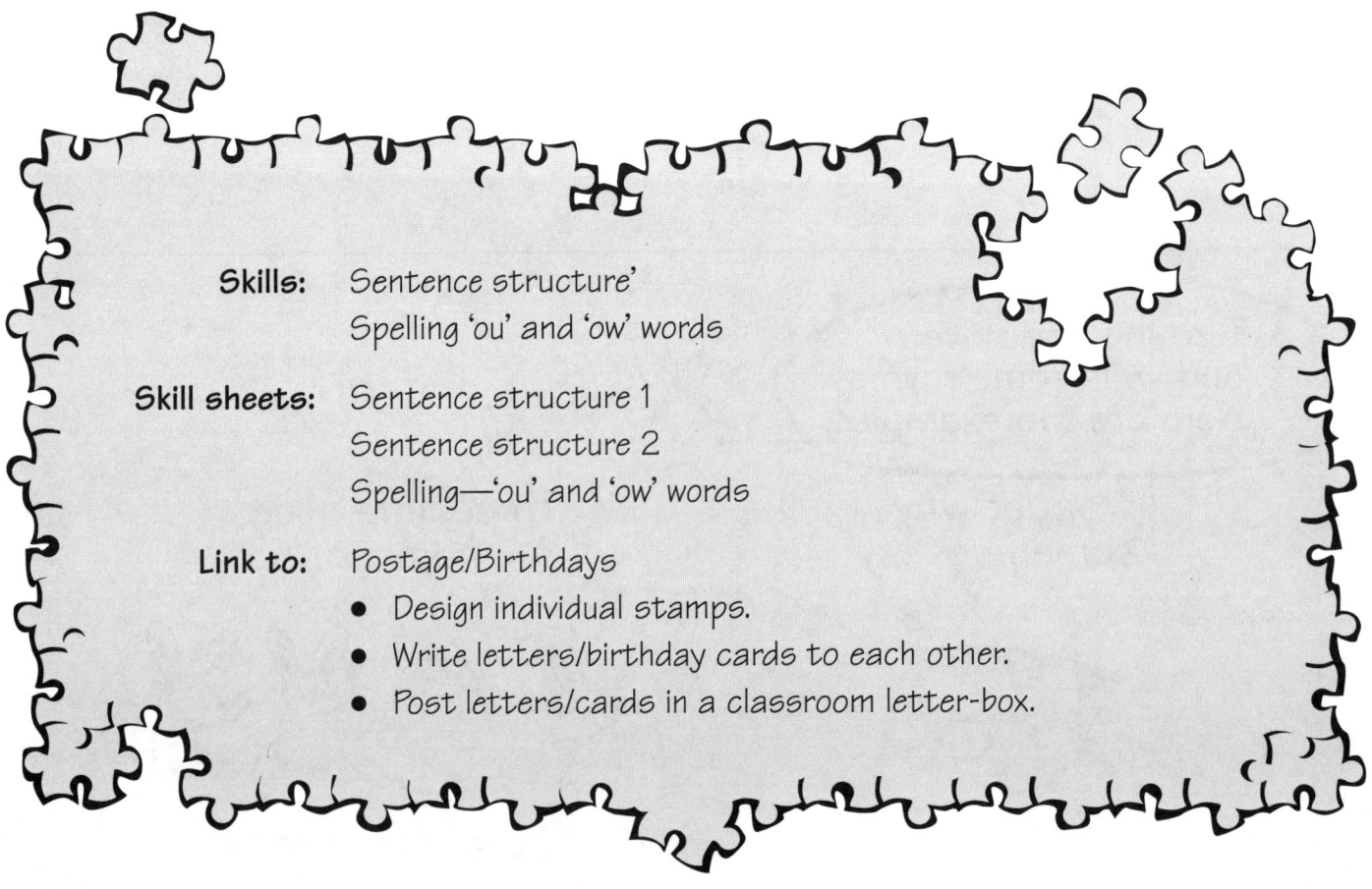

Skills: Sentence structure'
Spelling 'ou' and 'ow' words

Skill sheets: Sentence structure 1
Sentence structure 2
Spelling—'ou' and 'ow' words

Link to: Postage/Birthdays
- Design individual stamps.
- Write letters/birthday cards to each other.
- Post letters/cards in a classroom letter-box.

THE PARCEL

ORAL STAGE

- Recite the poem to the class.
- Recite the poem to the class again.

  Nominate a child to mime the actions.

- Recite the poem together with the class.

  Invite all the children to stand and mime the actions.

- Say the first word of each line.

  Ask the children to complete each line.

Discussion: Surprises.

- Recite the poem together with the class.
- Ask the children to imagine the contents of a parcel.

  One child whispers her or his contents to the teacher. The rest are allowed five questions to guess the parcel's contents.

- Ask questions at appropriate levels:

  1. What was in the letter-box?
  2. What colour was the parcel?
  3. Why did I shake it?
  4. What does 'tightly bound' mean?
  5. What else can be 'tightly bound'?
  6. Why do people whisper?

- Divide the class into two groups.

  Group 1 says the poem. Group 2 claps. Reverse roles.

THE PARCEL

WRITTEN STAGE

Visual presentation: Teacher/child uses a pointer and recites the poem, substituting or omitting words and/or consonants. Nominate a child to isolate and correct words.

Base Level

- Copy and distribute the Sentence Structure 1 sheet (page 55).

  Ask the children to write the line endings in the space provided.

  Children create a booklet using the copy of the poem. Have one line per page.

  Children circle all the 'ou' and 'ow' words in the poem.

Middle Level

- Copy and distribute the 'ou'/'ow' Spelling sheet (page 57).

  Children fill the gaps with an appropriate word from the list.

  On the back of the sheet children write a sentence for each unused word.

- Copy and distribute the Sentence Structure 2 sheet (page 56).

  Children write three different endings for each beginning.

Advanced Level

- Point out the sentence structure and pattern of the poem.

  Ask the children to rewrite the poem, changing as many words as possible, but maintaining the pattern.

  Each child reproduces their new poem in booklet form.

- Make available classroom books and dictionaries for children to use.

  Children research 'ou' (as in shout) and 'ow' (as in cow) words. Use classroom books as a resource. List all the words in dictionary order.

THE PARCEL
Reproducible Skill Sheet 1— Sentence Structure 1

Name: _____

1. Write the ending of each line from the poem.
2. Circle all the 'ou' words in the poem.
3. Circle all the 'ow' words in the poem.
4. Use each line to make up a booklet.

The Parcel

I walked to the letter-box
And what did I see?
A big brown parcel just for me.
I shook it.
I poked it.
I yelled "Yippee!"

Whisper what you think I found
In that parcel,
Tightly bound.

I walked _____
And what _____
A big _____
I _____
I _____
I yelled, " _____
Whisper what you think _____
In _____
Tightly _____

©N.Cahill & M.Pratt, *Literacy Skills Through Rhyme and Rhythm*, Oxford University Press, 1996.

THE PARCEL
Reproducible Skill Sheet 2 — Sentence Structure 2

Name: _____

Write three different endings for each beginning.

I walked _____

I whispered _____

I shook _____

I poked _____

I yelled _____

A big _____

THE PARCEL
Reproducible Skill Sheet 3 — Spelling 'ou' and 'ow' words

Name: _____

- Fill the gaps with a word from the box.

found	sound	out	brown	growl	mountain
shout	mouse	owl		clown	cow
frown	around	bounce	crown		down

Colour each word in the box as you use it.

1 My mum _____ my lost lunch box.

2 The teacher whispered, "Don't make a _____."

3 My dad has _____ hair and a brown beard.

4 Ann saw a funny _____ at the circus.

5 The _____ squeaked and ran off with the cheese.

6 A dragon lives on top of the _____ .

7 Did you hear the bear _____ at the zoo?

8 At the pool I love going _____ the water slide.

9 Tim ran _____ the park with his dog.

10 "Moo," said the _____ . "Come and milk me now."

Turn the sheet over and write a sentence for each word left over in the box.

©N.Cahill & M.Pratt, Literacy Skills Through Rhyme and Rhythm, Oxford University Press, 1996.

AS I WAS

As I was going out one day
    My head fell off and rolled away.
But when I saw that it was gone,
    I picked it up and put it on.

And when I got into the street
    A fellow cried: "Look at your feet!"
I looked at them and sadly said:
    "I've left them both asleep in bed!"

Anonymous

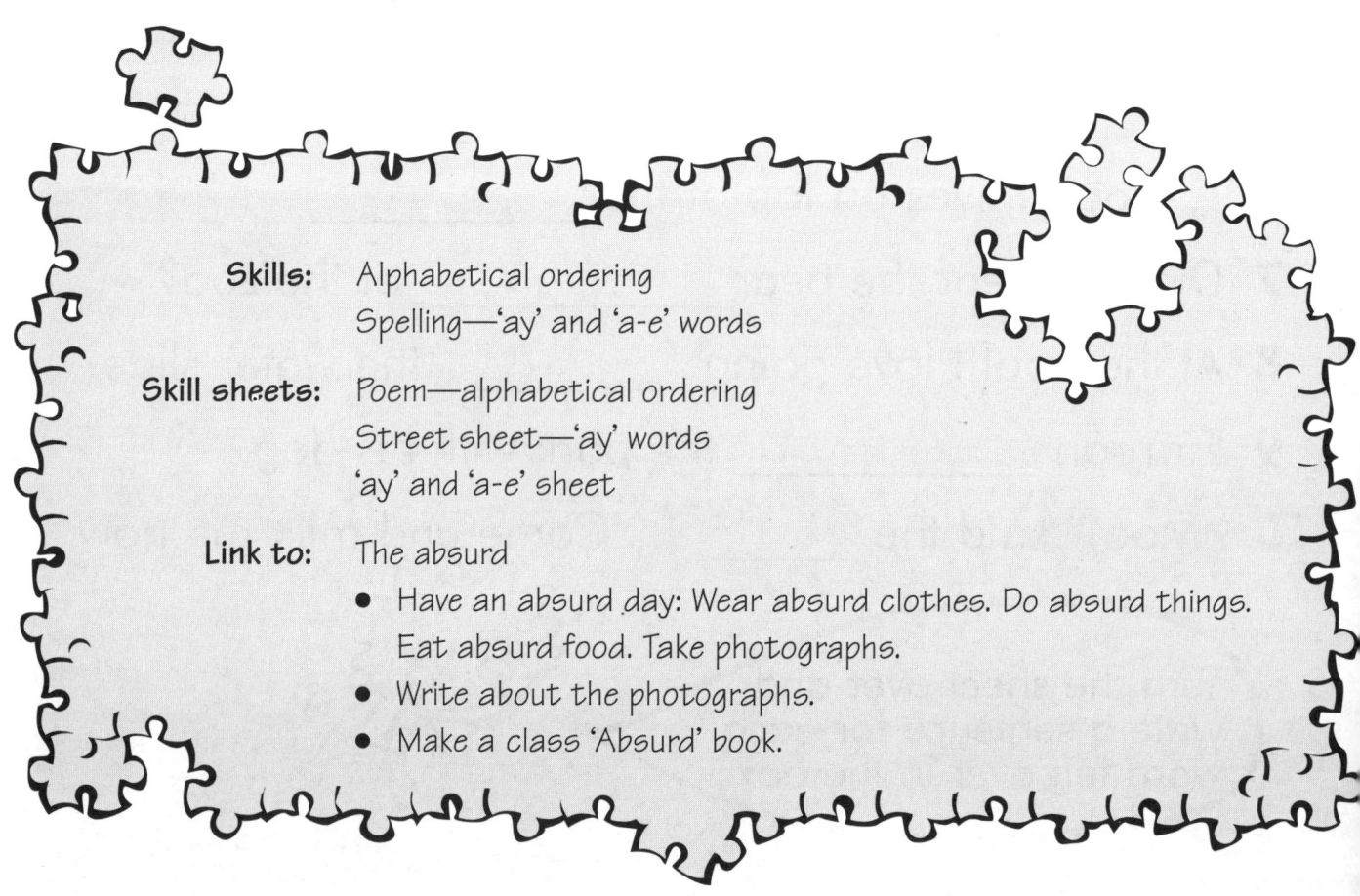

Skills:	Alphabetical ordering
	Spelling—'ay' and 'a-e' words
Skill sheets:	Poem—alphabetical ordering
	Street sheet—'ay' words
	'ay' and 'a-e' sheet
Link to:	The absurd

- Have an absurd day: Wear absurd clothes. Do absurd things. Eat absurd food. Take photographs.
- Write about the photographs.
- Make a class 'Absurd' book.

ORAL STAGE

- Recite the poem to the class.
- Recite the poem again, this time tapping out the main beat in each line.

  The children tap along with the teacher.
- Recite lines 1 and 2.

  Ask the children to repeat these lines.
- Recite lines 3 and 4, and so on.

  Ask the children to repeat after the teacher.

Discussion: Way-out things that could happen.

- Recite the poem together with the class.
- Ask questions at appropriate levels:
  1. What happened to the person's head?
  2. Where did the person leave his or her feet?
  3. What did the person do with his/her head when it fell off?
  4. Why did the fellow cry out?
  5. How would you feel if your head fell off?
  6. How would you manage if you had no feet?
- The class recites the poem while two children dramatise the actions.
- Organise children in pairs. They stand and face each other.

  The class recites the poem, clapping their partner's hands on the main beat. Alternate the left and right hands.

AS I WAS

WRITTEN STAGE

Visual presentation: Teacher/child uses a pointer and recites the poem, substituting or omitting words and/or consonants. Nominate a child to isolate and correct words.

Brainstorm 'ay' and 'a-e' words.

Base Level

- Hand out a copy of the poem to each child (page 61).

   Ask the children to circle the last word in each line and then list the words alphabetically.

   Children draw the person in the poem looking sad, and write the words the person said underneath the picture.

- Copy and distribute the Street sheet (page 62).

   Children write a different 'ay' word in each street sign.

Middle Level

- Hand out a copy of the poem to each child (page 61).

   Using only the first verse, children list every word in alphabetical order.

   The children make a comic strip of the poem, drawing a frame for each line. They write each line under its frame.

- Copy and distribute the 'ay/a-e' word sheet (page 63).

   Wordbuilding: The children follow the instructions to build new words.

   Children choose a few words from the categories to write into one sentence.

Advanced Level

- Discuss 'ay' and 'a-e' words.

   Ask the children to list 'ay' and 'a-e' words of one, two and three syllables.

   Children work in pairs or individually to create a comic strip using some of these words.

- Children write a different second verse containing exclamation and quotation marks.

AS I WAS

Name: _____

As I was going out one day
　My head fell off and rolled away.
But when I saw that it was gone,
　I picked it up and put it on.

And when I got into the street
　A fellow cried: "Look at your feet!"
I looked at them and sadly said:
　"I've left them both asleep in bed!"

AS I WAS
Reproducible Skill Sheet 2 — 'ay' words

Name: _____

Write an 'ay' word in each sign you can see along the street.

AS I WAS — 'ay' and 'a-e' words

Reproducible Skill Sheet 3

Name: _____

1. Build each word as shown.
2. Use some of these words to write in one sentence.

	Add 'ing'	Add 'ed'
play		
sway		
pray		
replay		
stay		
spray		

	Drop the 'e' and add 'ing'	Add 'd'
hate		
wave		
blame		
taste		
bake		
fade		

JUNK

We made this thing of jumbly junk
Four legs, three arms, six eyes.
And when we'd hammered forty nails
It moved to our surprise.

It walked about and creaked and clicked
And even shook its head,
But when it spoke with rusty voice
"Goodbye" was all it said.

Libby Hathorn

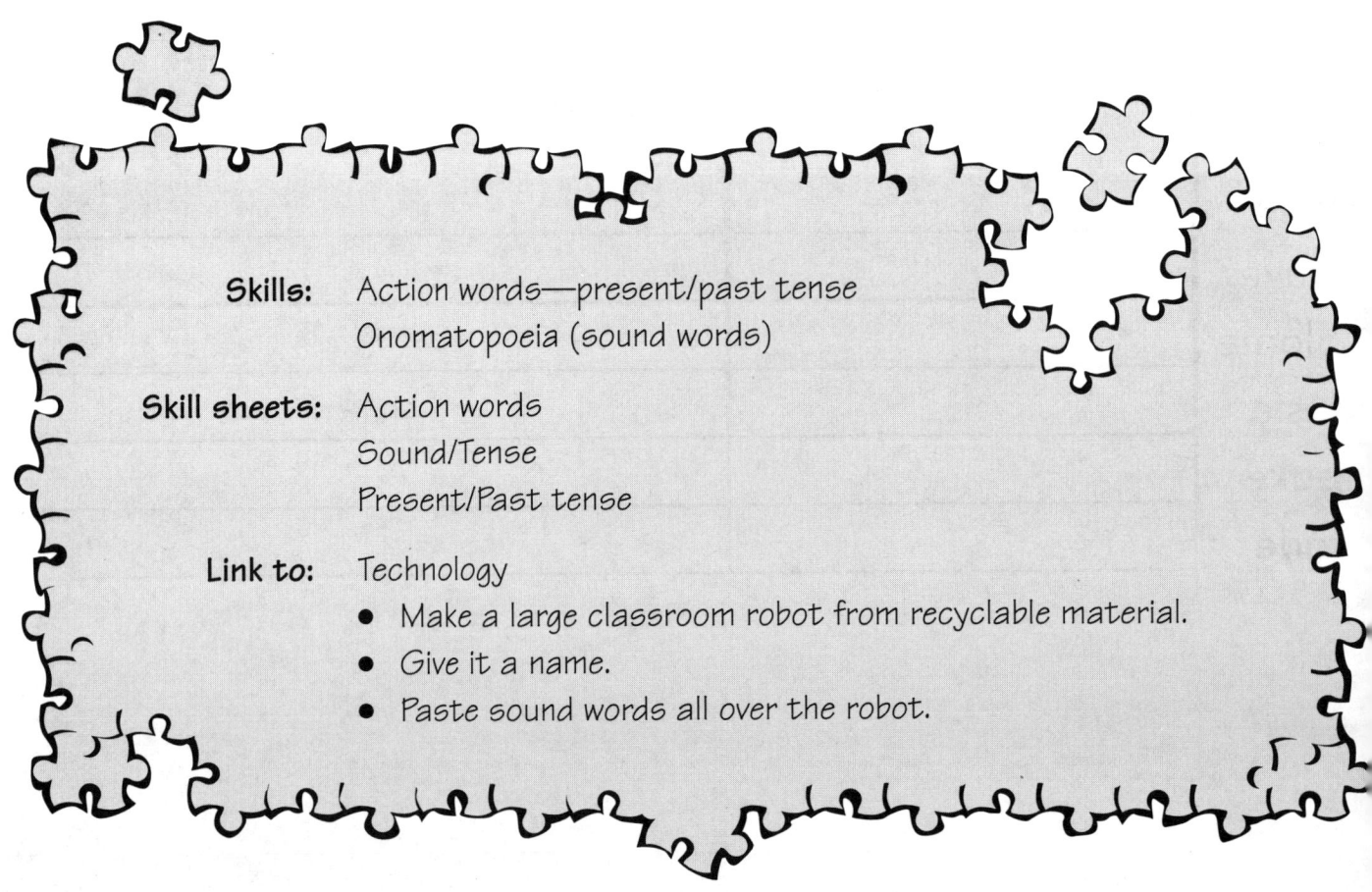

Skills:	Action words—present/past tense
	Onomatopoeia (sound words)
Skill sheets:	Action words
	Sound/Tense
	Present/Past tense
Link to:	Technology

- Make a large classroom robot from recyclable material.
- Give it a name.
- Paste sound words all over the robot.

ORAL STAGE

- Recite the poem to the class.
- Recite the poem again.

  The children join in at the numbers 'four', 'three', 'six', 'forty'.

- Recite the poem again.

  The children clap on every action word.

- Recite the poem again, this time substituting the present tense with its past tense: make (made), move (moved), creak (creaked), shake (shook), say (said), hammer (hammered), walk (walked), click (clicked), speak (spoke).

  Nominate a child or ask the whole class to make an instant correction of the past tense each time.

Discussion: Uses for junk.

- Recite the poem together with the class.
- Ask questions at appropriate levels:
  1. How many nails were hammered?
  2. What did the junk robot say when it spoke?
  3. What sound did its voice make? Demonstrate.
  4. How many different things did it do?
  5. Where do you think the junk robot might go?
  6. What do you think it might do?
- The class recites the poem while a nominated child dramatises the actions.
- The whole class stands up and recites the poem with actions.

JUNK

WRITTEN STAGE

Visual presentation: Teacher/child uses a pointer and recites the poem, substituting or omitting words and/or consonants. Nominate a child to isolate and correct words.

All Levels

- Introduce onomatopoeia. Brainstorm sound words for robots.
- List words on a large sheet, for example:

  | grind | rattle | bubble | clatter | click | squeak | scrape |
  | scratch | thump | crunch | scrunch | snort | clash | jangle |

Base Level

- Copy and distribute the Action Word sheet (page 67).

  Ask the children to circle the action words. They write some of the action words in sentences.

  Each child draws another robot on the back of their Action Word sheet and fills it in with words from the class brainstorm list.

- Children write a 'noisy sentence' about a robot, using the brainstorm list.

Middle Level

- Copy and distribute the Sound/Tense Word sheet (page 68).

  Children write the past tense under the given present tense. Then they use the past tense in imaginative sentences.

- Each child writes a short story about a robot. They may use the brainstorm list to help them. Illustrate the story.

Advanced Level

- Display a copy of the poem.

  Ask the children to change the poem by making all the action words different. They must maintain the past tense and rhyming pattern.

- Copy and distribute Present/Past Tense sheet (page 69).

  The children list objects which make sounds. They add present/past tense sound words.

- Children write a robot story of about one page. Instruct them to neatly tear the page across the middle and exchange the bottom half with a partner. Children write the first half of the story, this time to fit with the facts on the second half they have received.

JUNK
Reproducible Skill Sheet 1— **Action words**

Name: _____

1 Circle all the action words.
2 Write some of the action words in sentences below.

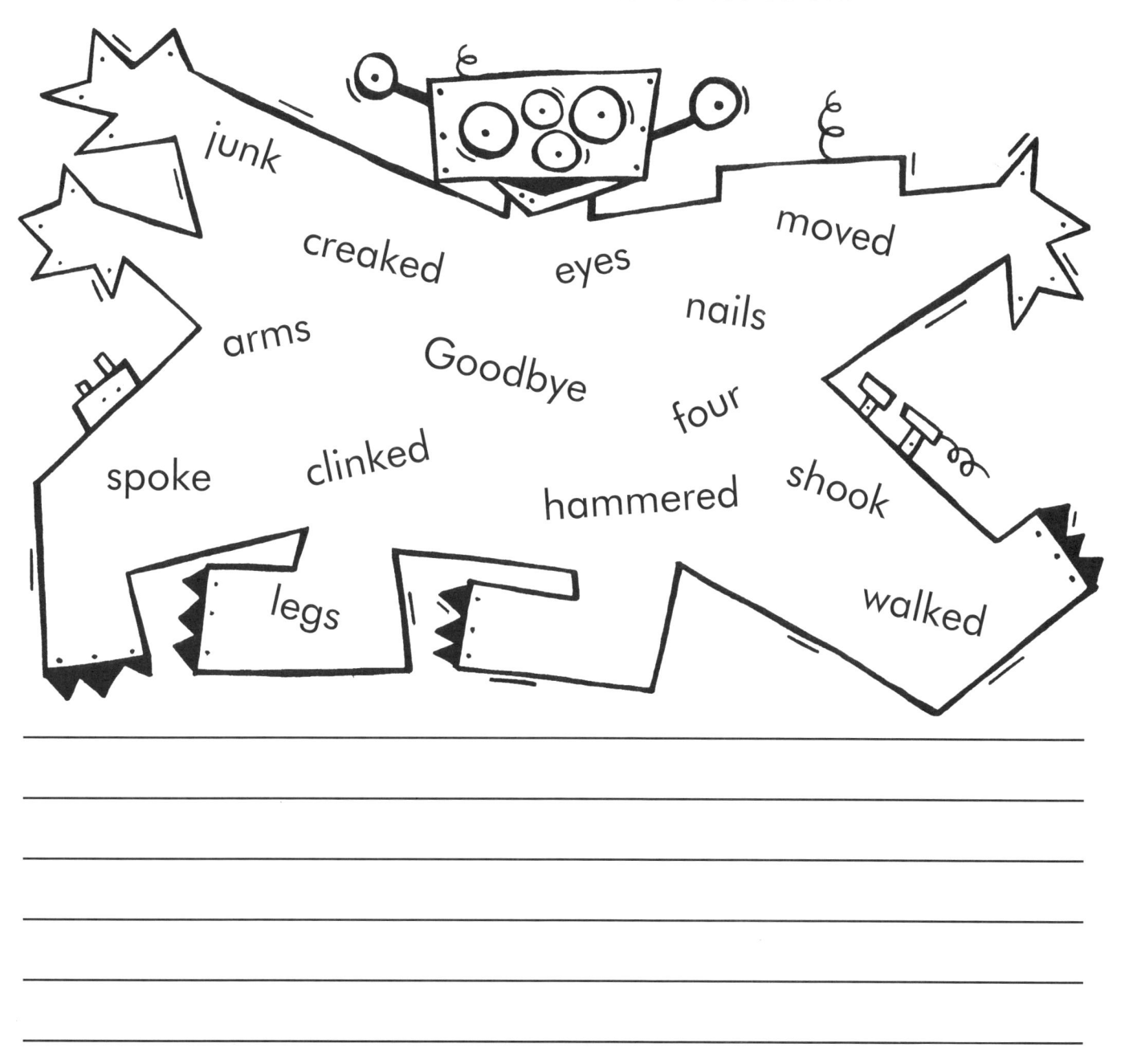

junk
creaked
eyes
moved
arms
Goodbye
nails
four
spoke
clinked
hammered
shook
legs
walked

_____
_____
_____
_____
_____
_____

©N.Cahill & M.Pratt, *Literacy Skills Through Rhyme and Rhythm*, Oxford University Press, 1996.

JUNK
Reproducible Skill Sheet 2 — Sound/Tense words

Name: _____

1. Write the past tense of each word under the given present tense. The first one is done for you.
2. Use the past tense word in an interesting sentence. The first one is done for you.

creak creaked	Slowly, slowly the door creaked open.
click _____	
rattle _____	
thump _____	
bubble _____	
hammer _____	

JUNK
Reproducible Skill Sheet 3 — **Present/Past tense**

Name: _____

1 List things which make sounds in the 'Object' column.
2 Write present and past tense sound words for the object.

Object	SOUND WORDS	
	Present	**Past**
thunder	rumbles	rumbled

IF YOU SHOULD MEET A CROCODILE

If you should meet a crocodile
Don't take a stick and poke him.
Ignore the welcome in his smile,
Be careful not to stroke him.
For as he sleeps a long long while
He gets a lot lot thinner.
So when you meet a crocodile
He's ready for his dinner.

Anonymous

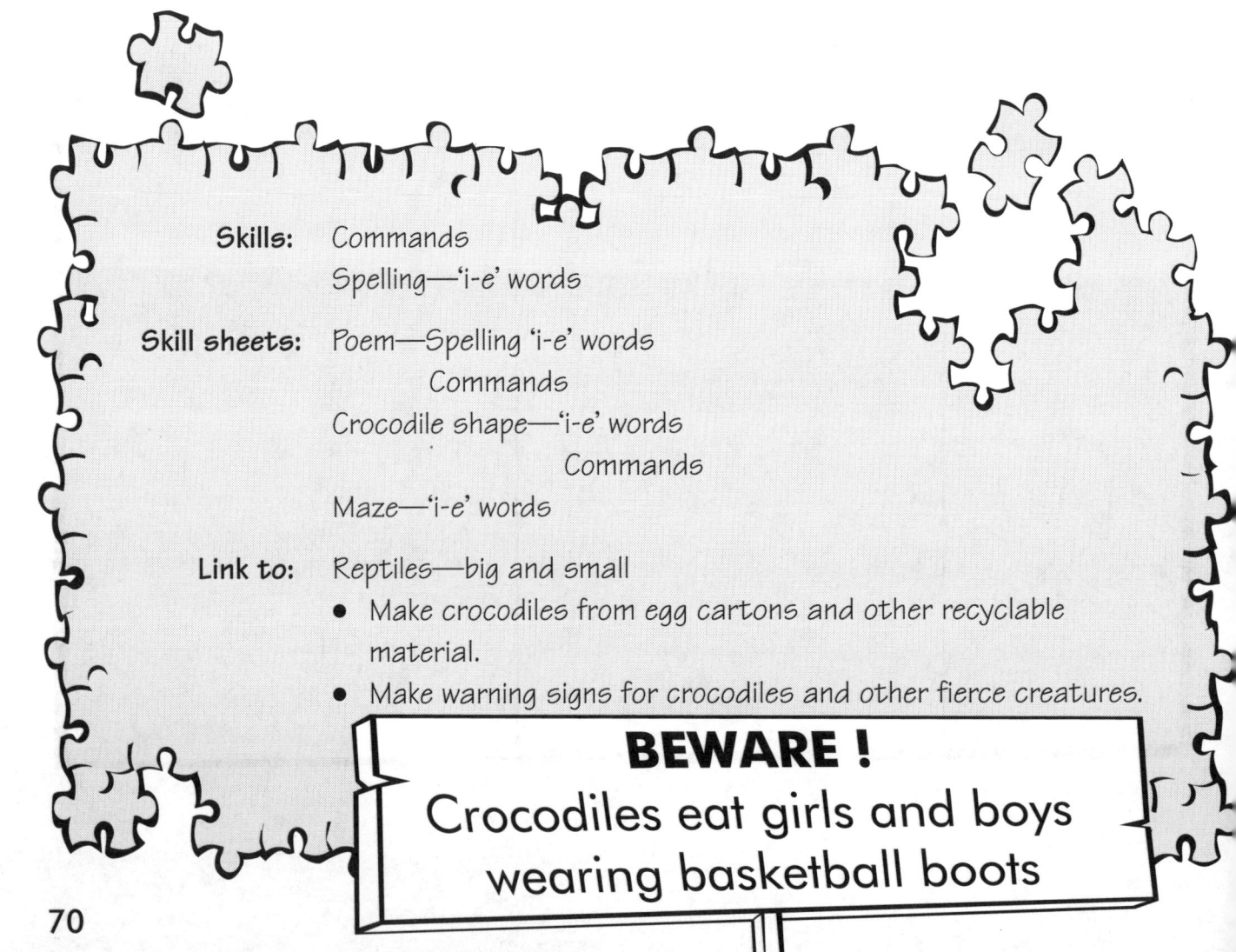

Skills: Commands
Spelling—'i-e' words

Skill sheets: Poem—Spelling 'i-e' words
Commands
Crocodile shape—'i-e' words
Commands
Maze—'i-e' words

Link to: Reptiles—big and small
- Make crocodiles from egg cartons and other recyclable material.
- Make warning signs for crocodiles and other fierce creatures.

BEWARE !
Crocodiles eat girls and boys wearing basketball boots

IF YOU SHOULD MEET A CROCODILE

ORAL STAGE

- Recite the poem to the class.
- Recite the poem again.

  Ask the children to rap their knuckles on the table to the main beat.

- Recite the poem together with the class.

  Nominate a child to use the pointer and tap the floor to the main beat.

- Recite lines 1 to 6, while the children rap their knuckles on the table.

  The children say lines 7 and 8.

- Recite lines 1 to 4.

  Children say lines 5 to 8 while continuing to rap.

- Recite the poem, changing each 'ile' word to a nonsense rhyming word.

  The children rap their knuckles on the table each time they hear a changed word. Nominate a child to correct the word.

Discussion: Dangerous creatures—big and small.

- Recite the poem together with the class.
- Ask questions at appropriate levels:

  1. Is it all right to stroke a crocodile?
  2. Why/Why not?
  3. What happens to the crocodile while he sleeps? Why?
  4. What kind of smile does the crocodile have?
  5. How many ways could a crocodile hurt you?
  6. What would it be like if crocodiles were friendly? How would we need to change the poem?

- Ask the children to recite the poem. Nominate two children to mime all the actions.

IF YOU SHOULD MEET A CROCODILE

WRITTEN STAGE

Visual presentation: Teacher/child uses a pointer and recites the poem, substituting or omitting words and/or consonants. Nominate a child to isolate and correct words.

Base Level

- Hand out a copy of the poem to each child (page 73) and copies of the Crocodile sheet (page 74).

    Ask the children to write over each 'i-e' word in the poem.

    Children write the 'i-e' words around the crocodile shape.

- Discuss commands.

    Children find the commands in the poem and write over the commands on the poem sheet. They write them out and illustrate.

Middle Level

- Copy and distribute the Crocodile sheet (page 74).

    The children list the three commands in the poem and think of three more.

    Children write some of these commands around the crocodile shape.

    Children create the outline of a crocodile shape using 'i-e' words.

Advanced Level

- Copy and distribute the Crocodile Maze sheet (page 75).

    Ask the children to solve the maze using the word clues.

    Children devise their own maze, using different command words in their instructions and their clues.

- Children create a 'dangerous animal' shape poem containing at least ten 'i-e' words.

IF YOU SHOULD MEET A CROCODILE

Reproducible Skill Sheet 1— 'i-e' words and commands

Name: _____

1 Find the 'i-e' words and write over them.

2 Find the commands and write over them. Make an illustration of each command.

If you should meet a crocodile
Don't take a stick and poke him.
Ignore the welcome in his smile,
Be careful not to stroke him.
For as he sleeps a long long while
He gets a lot lot thinner.
So when you meet a crocodile
He's ready for his dinner.

IF YOU SHOULD MEET A CROCODILE
Reproducible Skill Sheet 2 — 'i-e' words and commands

Name: _____

IF YOU SHOULD MEET A CROCODILE
Reproducible Skill Sheet 3 — 'i-e' words

Name: _____

1. Read the first clue on the word list.
2. Find the matching answer on the maze.
3. Colour that part of the path.
4. Continue through the clues until the correct path home is completely coloured.

Word list clues

1. do this when you're happy
2. like an alligator
3. opposite of narrow
4. a heap
5. angry
6. a snake
7. to do with the sea
8. partner of the bridegroom
9. rhymes with 'stride'
10. horrible
11. a distance
12. act without speaking

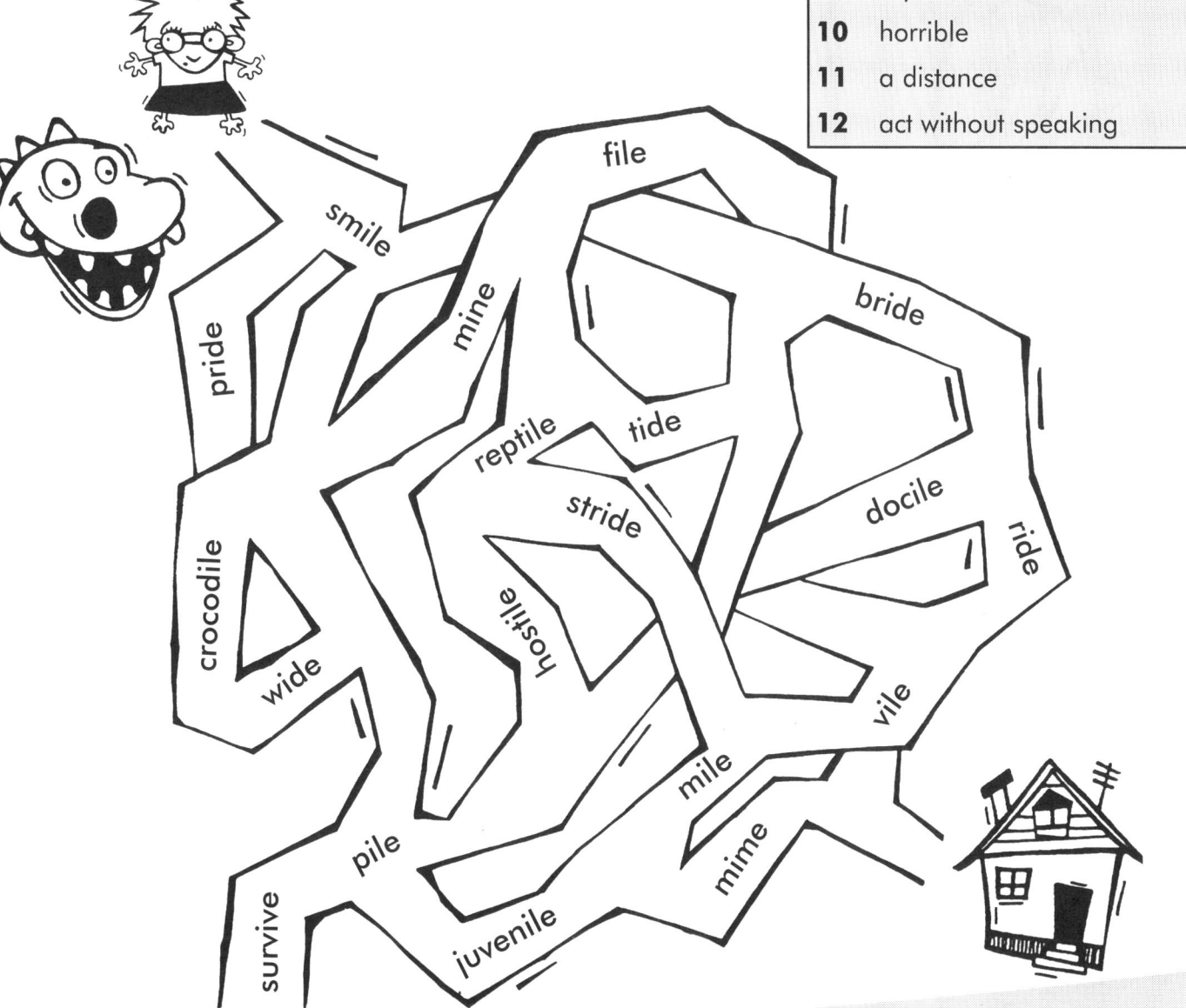

Maze words: smile, file, pride, mine, bride, reptile, tide, docile, stride, ride, crocodile, hostile, wide, vile, pile, mile, mime, survive, juvenile

©N.Cahill & M.Pratt, *Literacy Skills Through Rhyme and Rhythm*, Oxford University Press, 1996.

BRENDA BAKER

Brenda Baker, quite ill-bred,
Used to cuddle fish in bed.
Tuna, trout and conger-eels,
Salmon, sole and sometimes seals.
Barracuda, bream and bass,
She cuddled them, until — alas!
One unforgotten Friday night
She slept with two piranhas,
And, being rather impolite,
They ate her best pyjamas!

Doug MacLeod

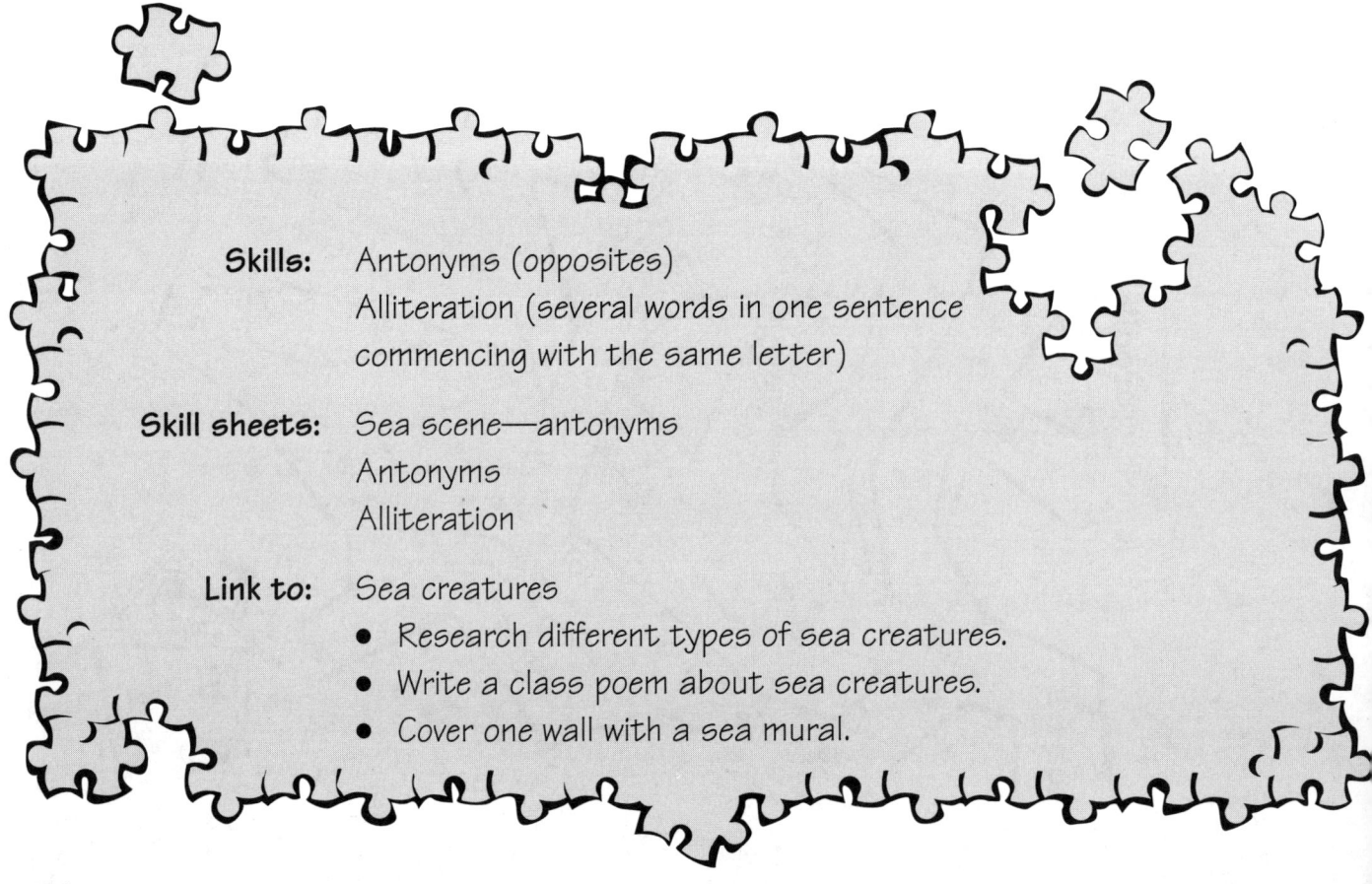

Skills:	Antonyms (opposites)
	Alliteration (several words in one sentence commencing with the same letter)
Skill sheets:	Sea scene—antonyms
	Antonyms
	Alliteration
Link to:	Sea creatures
	• Research different types of sea creatures.
	• Write a class poem about sea creatures.
	• Cover one wall with a sea mural.

BRENDA BAKER

ORAL STAGE

- Recite the poem to the class.
- Recite the poem again, this time pausing before interest words, e.g. 'fish', 'cuddled', 'Friday', 'piranhas', 'pyjamas'.

  The children nominate the appropriate word.

- Name each fish in poem order.

  The children clap the syllables for each name.

- Recite the poem, substituting opposite words: ill-bred/well-bred, unforgotten/forgotten, slept/woke, best/worst, impolite/polite and so on.

  Ask the children to clap each time an opposite word is said. Children say the correct word.

Discussion: Why is this poem absurd? Other absurd situations.

- Recite the poem together with the class.
- Ask questions at appropriate levels:
  1. What did Brenda do with the fish?
  2. Name some of the different fish?
  3. Would you find it difficult to cuddle fish? Why? Why not?
  4. What kind of manners did the piranhas have?
  5. How could you give an everyday situation an absurd ending?
  6. Can you describe an unforgettable experience?
- Divide the class into two groups.

  Group 1 chants 'splash, splash, splash, splash' to each line as Group 2 recites the poem. Reverse the procedure.

BRENDA BAKER

WRITTEN STAGE

Visual presentation: Teacher/child uses a pointer and recites the poem, substituting or omitting words and/or consonants. Nominate a child to isolate and correct words.

Base Level

- Display a copy of the poem.

  The children write out the poem. Then they circle the name of each fish and write them down. They add an action word beginning with the same letter, e.g. tuna/toss, sole/sing.

- Copy and distribute the Sea Scene sheet (page 79).

  Ask the children to write the correct opposites in the appropriate boxes.

Middle Level

- Copy and distribute the Antonym Words sheet (page 80).

  Children write the antonym beside each word, then write some words in sentences to show their meaning.

  Children write a sentence about each fish in the poem. Every word in the sentence must start with the same letter, e.g. 'The tuna tickled their toes.'

- Copy and distribute the Alliteration sheet (page 81).

  Ask the children to write descriptive sentences using alliteration, e.g. 'Brenda's brown boat is bouncing on the blue waves.'

Advanced Level

- Display a copy of the poem.

  Ask the children to rewrite the poem, substituting other creatures for fish. The poem must contain examples of alliteration and opposites.

  Children work in pairs to create an absurd underwater scene. Then list words, with opposites, from the scene. They write these words in code or jumbled, placing them appropriately in the underwater scene.

  They exchange coded sheets with another group and decode the exchanged sheets.

BRENDA BAKER
Reproducible Skill Sheet 1— **Antonyms**

Name: _____

Write the correct words and their opposites in the sea scene.

shallow	deep	rough	smooth	sharp
blunt	hot	cold	happy	sad

©N.Cahill & M.Pratt, *Literacy Skills Through Rhyme and Rhythm*, Oxford University Press, 1996.

BRENDA BAKER
Reproducible Skill Sheet 2 — Antonyms

Name: _____

Write the opposite for each word and then use some to make up interesting sentences.

Word	Opposite
polite	
forgotten	
shout	
laugh	
dirty	
loud	
hate	
poor	
depart	
answer	
difficult	
ancient	
skinny	
sweet	
war	

My sentences

_____
_____
_____
_____

BRENDA BAKER
Reproducible Skill Sheet 3 — **Alliteration**

Name: _____

You are a whale circling a small fishing boat on the ocean.

1. Write sentences in each box.
2. Remember to use alliterations.

Describe the boat.

[ ]

Describe the people on board. How do they look? What are they doing?

[ ]

Describe the scene one hour later.

[ ]

How many alliterations did you write?

©N.Cahill & M.Pratt, *Literacy Skills Through Rhyme and Rhythm*, Oxford University Press, 1996.

ODE TO AN EXTINCT DINOSAUR

Iguanadon, I loved you,
With all your spiky scales,
Your massive jaws,
Impressive claws
And teeth like horseshoe nails.

Iguanadon, I loved you.
It moved me close to tears
When I first read
That you've been dead
For ninety million years.

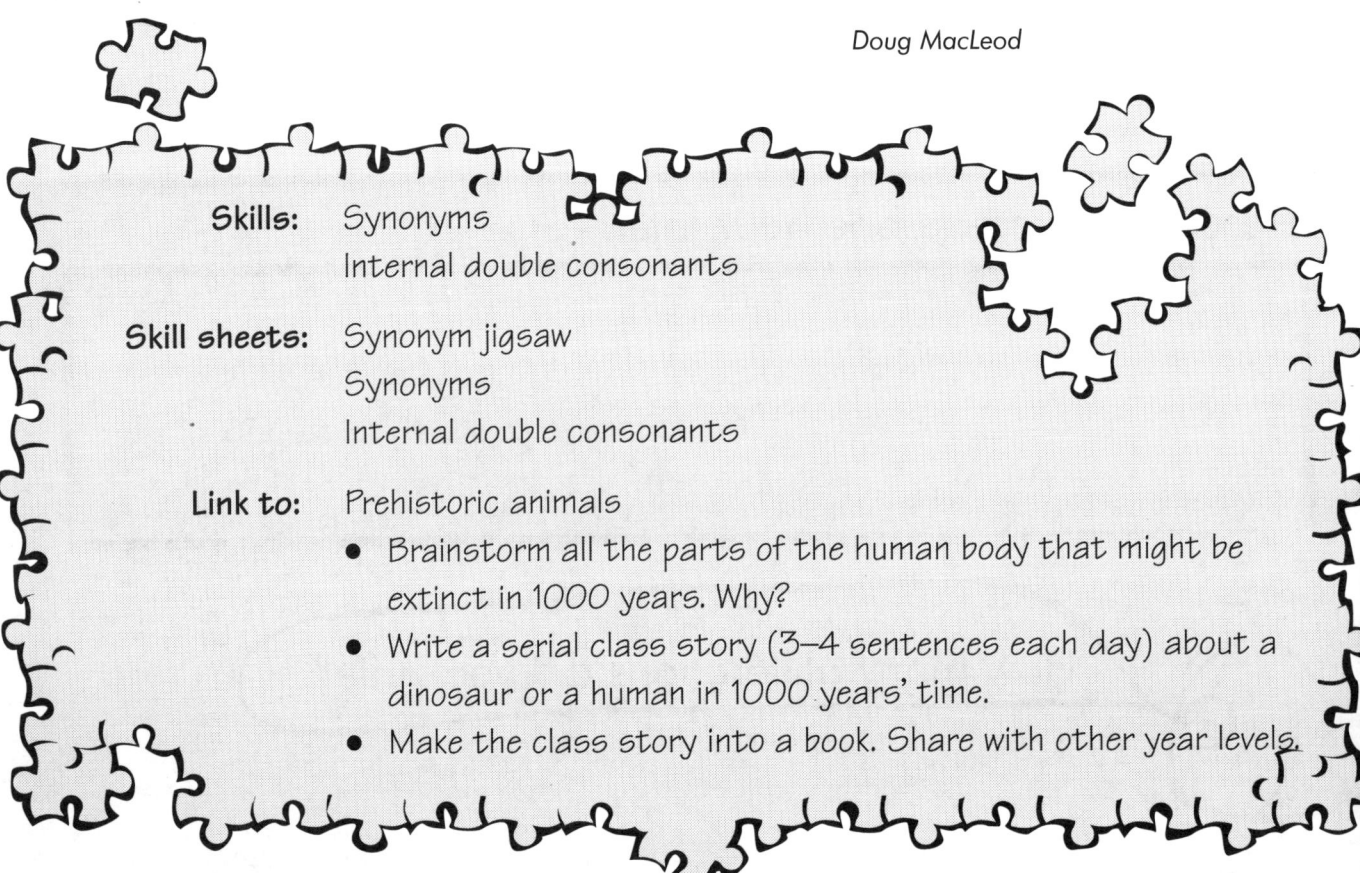

Doug MacLeod

Skills: Synonyms
Internal double consonants

Skill sheets: Synonym jigsaw
Synonyms
Internal double consonants

Link to: Prehistoric animals
- Brainstorm all the parts of the human body that might be extinct in 1000 years. Why?
- Write a serial class story (3–4 sentences each day) about a dinosaur or a human in 1000 years' time.
- Make the class story into a book. Share with other year levels.

ODE TO AN EXTINCT DINOSAUR

ORAL STAGE

- Recite the poem to the class.
- Recite the poem again.

  At the appropriate places, children mime actions for 'massive jaws', 'impressive claws'.

- Recite the poem again while selected children mime all the actions in the poem.
- Say the following words:
  'claws'
  'impressive'
  'horseshoe'
  'massive'
  'loved
  'Iguanadon'.

  Children repeat each word, clapping the correct number of syllables.

Discussion: Do animals have to be beautiful to be loved?

- Recite the poem together with the class, miming the actions.
- Ask questions at appropriate levels:
  1. What were the dinosaur's teeth like?
  2. Were his jaws big or small?
  3. Why was the poet 'moved to tears'?
  4. What would move you to tears?
  5. Why did the poet use the word 'extinct'?
  6. Did he need to use 'extinct'?
- Divide the class into two groups.

  Group 1 recites the first verse as Group 2 mimes the actions. Groups reverse roles for the second verse.

ODE TO AN EXTINCT DINOSAUR

WRITTEN STAGE

Visual presentation: Teacher/child uses a pointer and recites the poem, substituting or omitting words and/or consonants. Nominate a child to isolate and correct word.

Base Level

- Copy and distribute the Synonym Jigsaw sheet (page 85).

  The children cut out the letters and remake the words.

- Display a copy of the poem.

  Ask the children to write out the poem. Then colour words with internal double consonants.

- Supply blank sheets for drawing.

  Children draw a large dinosaur outline and fill the shape with their favourite words from the poem.

Middle Level

- Copy and distribute the Synonyms sheet (page 86).

  Children fill the gaps with appropriate synonyms for 'extremely big'. Ask them to write a similar short story, using these and other synonyms.

  For each word in the boxes displayed on the sheet, children must write three synonyms.

- Copy and distribute the Internal Double Consonants sheet (page 87).

  Children write a short story about a dinosaur, using the words listed and ending with the sentence supplied.

Advanced Level

- Display books on dinosaurs and other prehistoric creatures.

  Children list at least seven parts of a dinosaur's body. Add one word to describe each part, e.g. Teeth: pointy. They add at least one synonym for each describing word, e.g. Teeth: pointy, sharp.

  Ask the children to write an ode to a dinosaur in which they use at least five words containing internal double consonants.

ODE TO AN EXTINCT DINOSAUR
Reproducible Skill Sheet 1— **Synonym 1**

Name: _____

1 Cut out the jumbled jigsaw letters.
2 Paste them in correct order alongside the matching word.

big	_____
massive	_____
large	_____
huge	_____

s	i	v	s	e	a	m
e	h	u	g			
a	g	e	l	r		
g	b	i				

©N.Cahill & M.Pratt, *Literacy Skills Through Rhyme and Rhythm*, Oxford University Press, 1996.

ODE TO AN EXTINCT DINOSAUR
Reproducible Skill Sheet 2 — Synonyms 2

Name: _____

1 Fill in the gaps in the story with the words below.

I heard an _____ thump and looked out the window.

A _____ dinosaur was in my garden kicking my football.

He saw me, smiled and flashed his _____ teeth.

"Come and have a kick," he bellowed and stamped his _____ foot.

"I'm not allowed to play with dinosaurs," I squeaked.

"Oh drat!" he rumbled, and curling his _____ body into a _____ ball he rolled away.

| colossal | enormous | gigantic | massive | immense | huge |

2 Add three synonyms for each word.

small **talk** **spiky** **yell**

____   ____   ____   ____

____   ____   ____   ____

____   ____   ____   ____

3 Turn over and write a story using synonyms.

ODE TO AN EXTINCT DINOSAUR
Reproducible Skill Sheet 3 — Internal double consonants

Name: _____

1. Write a dinosaur story using some of the words below.
2. Finish your story with the sentence already written for you.

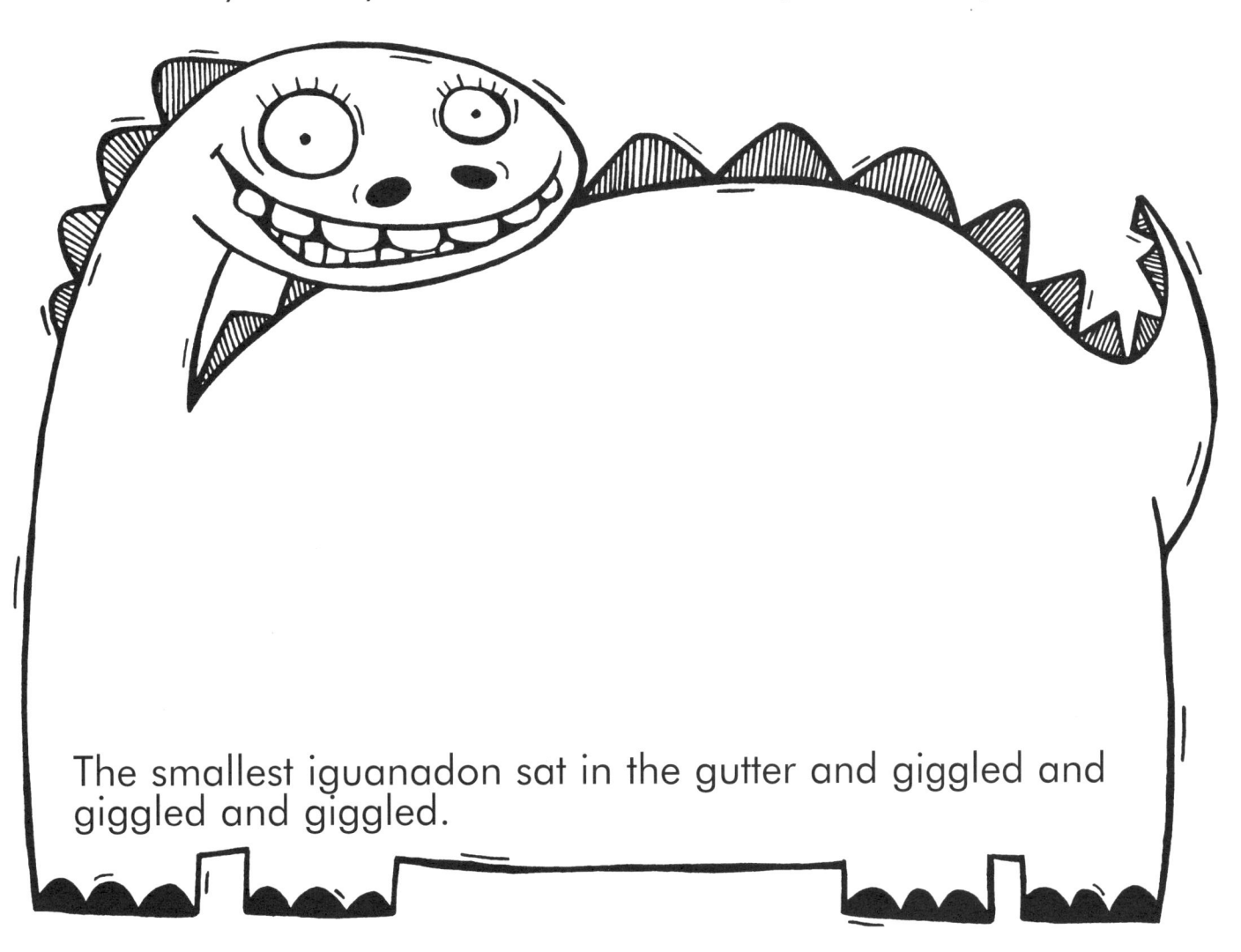

The smallest iguanadon sat in the gutter and giggled and giggled and giggled.

sniffle	mutter	puddle	rabbit
bottom	middle	butter	cannot
little	splutter	scatter	gallop
wriggle	bottle	ribbon	
bubble	muddle	woollen	

THE TEACHER TOOK MY TENNIS BALL

The teacher took my tennis ball
She took it for the day,
Just because it broke some glass
She said I couldn't play.

I'd like to try the same with her
When I think she goes too far —
"Miss Jones," I'd like to say to her,
"I'm going to take your car.
No Miss Jones, I'm sorry
You're not allowed to borrow —
But if you're really good
You'll get it back tomorrow!
Maybe."

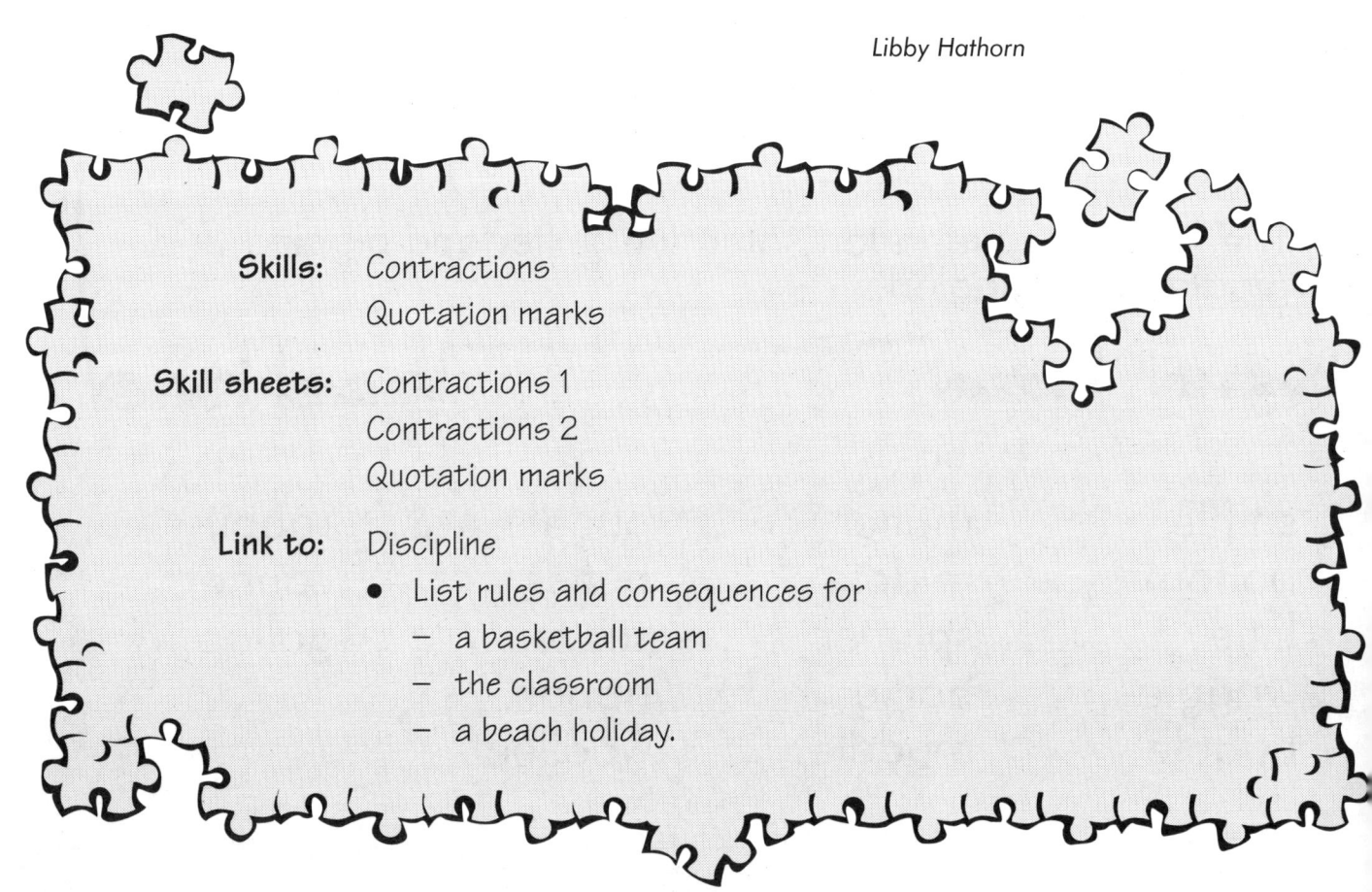

Libby Hathorn

Skills: Contractions
Quotation marks

Skill sheets: Contractions 1
Contractions 2
Quotation marks

Link to: Discipline
- List rules and consequences for
  - a basketball team
  - the classroom
  - a beach holiday.

THE TEACHER TOOK MY TENNIS BALL

ORAL STAGE

- Recite the poem, with expression, to the class.
- Recite the poem up to the word 'borrow'.

  The children recite the last three lines.
- Recite the poem, stopping at each contraction.

  Point to the class and have them say the contraction with emphasis.

Discussion: Emotions we experience when being disciplined.

- Recite the poem together with the class.
- Ask questions at appropriate levels:

  1   Why did the teacher take the tennis ball?

  2   How long was she going to keep it?

  3   How would you feel if you were the child?

  4   What would Miss Jones have to do to get her car back?

  5   How would you have handled the situation if you were Miss Jones and a child took your car?

  6   Should the punishment fit the crime?

- Recite the poem together with the class, up to 'far'.

  Nominate a child to recite and dramatise the remainder of the poem. Repeat with different children.

THE TEACHER TOOK MY TENNIS BALL

WRITTEN STAGE

Visual presentation: Teacher/child uses a pointer and recites the poem, substituting or omitting words and/or consonants. Nominate a child to isolate and correct words.

Base Level

- Display a copy of the poem.

  The children write the poem down and circle all the contractions.

  They mark all the quotation marks in red.

- Copy and distribute the Contractions 1 sheet (page 91).

  Ask the children to write the contraction for each group of words.

Middle Level

- Copy and distribute the Contractions 2 sheet (page 92).

  The children write the contractions and the words it represents in each box, using I, you, he/she, we, they where appropriate. Ask them to use some contractions in sentences about discipline (e.g. I'd like to go outside but my Mum won't let me).

  Children rewrite the poem using their own words for lines 1 and 3.

  Work in groups to make up posters using quotation marks and contractions (e.g. I yelled, "It's mine!"). Illustrate.

Advanced Level

- Copy and distribute the Quotation Marks sheet (page 93).

  Children follow the example to complete the sheet with their own scenarios.

  Children write a newspaper heading using quotation marks. Then they write a short article about the event.

  Children rewrite the poem describing another experience, either real or imaginary. They must use quotation marks and contractions.

THE TEACHER TOOK MY TENNIS BALL
Reproducible Skill Sheet 1— **Contractions**

Name: _____

Write the contractions for the word groups.

would
I would = I'd
you would =
he would =
we would =
they would =

am
I am =

are
you are =
we are =
they are =

will
I will =
you will =
she will =
we will =
you will =
they will =

is
he is =
she is =

©N.Cahill & M.Pratt, *Literacy Skills Through Rhyme and Rhythm*, Oxford University Press, 1996.

THE TEACHER TOOK MY TENNIS BALL
Reproducible Skill Sheet 2 — **Contractions**

Name: _____

Make contractions. Use: I you he/she we they

would	**are**
I'd = I would	
	have
is	
am	
	had
will/shall	

THE TEACHER TOOK MY TENNIS BALL
Reproducible Skill Sheet 3 — **Quotation marks**

Name: _____

Use the example to write your own description of events.
(Remember to use quotation marks.)

Action	Words spoken to teacher	Words spoken by teacher	Result
Miss Jones drove over Tim's cricket bat.	Tim yelled, "I'm going to take your car."	Miss Jones begged, "Please don't. I'll give you my mum's cricket bat."	Tim gets Miss Jones' mum's cricket bat. Miss Jones twitches when she sees cricket bats.

©N.Cahill & M.Pratt, *Literacy Skills Through Rhyme and Rhythm*, Oxford University Press, 1996.

CAR ATTACK

On last year's Halloween
A car hit Auntie Jean.
Unhinged by this attack,
My Auntie hit it back.
    She hit it with her handbag
And knocked it with her knee.
She socked it with a sandbag
And thumped it with a tree.
    On last year's Halloween
A car hit Auntie Jean.
And now, my Auntie's better
But the car is with the wrecker.

Doug MacLeod

Skills: Rhyming words
Compound words

Skill sheets: Compound words 1
Compound words 2
Crossword

Link to: Unusual people
- Discuss unusual people you know or have read about.
- Form small groups and write simple plays about unusual people.
- Present plays to class.

ORAL STAGE

- Recite the poem to the class.
- Recite the poem to the class again, this time patting your knees with both hands to the main beat of each line.
- Recite the poem to the class.

  This time the children pat their knees with both hands to the main beat of each line.
- Recite the poem, stopping before the last word of each line.

  Children complete the line.
- Divide the class into two groups.

  Group 1 chants the first word in each line. Group 2 chants the remainder of the line. Reverse the procedure.

Discussion: People like Auntie Jean.

- Recite the poem together with the class.
- Ask questions at appropriate levels.
  1. What hit Auntie Jean?
  2. Where is the car now?
  3. What is Halloween?
  4. What does 'unhinged' mean?
  5. Could this really happen?
  6. Why is this poem funny?
- Ask the children to recite the poem.

  Nominate children to dramatise the roles of Auntie and the car.
- The children recite the poem while marching on the spot to the main beat.

CAR ATTACK

WRITTEN STAGE

Visual presentation: Teacher/child uses a pointer and recites the poem, substituting or omitting words and/or consonants. Nominate a child to isolate and correct words.

Base Level

- Copy and distribute the Compound Words 1 sheet (page 97).

  The children make compound words from each group and write the new words in sentences. Illustrate.

- Display a copy of the poem.

  Children write out the poem and circle all the rhyming words in matching colours.

  Collect lists of rhyming words for 'Jean', 'knee' and 'back'.

Middle Level

- Display a copy of the poem.

  The children write out the poem and circle all the rhyming words. Ask them to list more rhyming words to match these.

- Copy and distribute the Compound Words 2 sheet (page 98).

  The children make compound words by guessing the first half and combining it with a word in the list of second halves. They write down their compound words and use them in sentences.

  Children write a poem about a car. Ask them to include some compound words.

Advanced Level

- Children work in pairs.

  Each child creates a wordsearch using only compound words. They exchange the puzzles for their partners to solve.

  Children complete an acrostic which describes the poem. Use the words UNHINGED or WRECKER.

- Copy and distribute the Crossword sheet (page 99).

  Four words from the poem can each be written twice in the crossword (i.e. better, with, thumped, socked). Children try to find them and complete the puzzle.

CAR ATTACK
Reproducible Skill Sheet 1— **Compound words**

Name: _____

1 Make compound words from a word in the first car and a word in the second car.

2 Put a line through each word as you use it and write the new word in the list. (See 'hand' plus 'bag'.)

3 Write the compound words in sentences and illustrate.

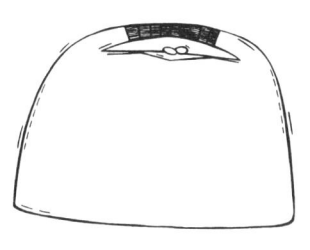

Compound words

1 handbag
2 _____
3 _____
4 _____
5 _____
6 _____
7 _____
8 _____
9 _____
10 _____
11 _____

First car: ship, door, snow, eye, fish, lip, sun, bee, tooth, ~~hand~~

Second car: stick, ache, lid, set, way, tank, hive, man, wreck, ~~bag~~

©N.Cahill & M.Pratt, *Literacy Skills Through Rhyme and Rhythm*, Oxford University Press, 1996.

CAR ATTACK
Reproducible Skill Sheet 2 — Compound words

Name: _____

1 Make compound words by guessing the first half and matching it with the second half.

2 Write the new word down.

3 Turn over and use these words in sentences.

	First half		Compound Words
1	t _ _ th	1	toothpaste
2	m _ _ n	2	_____
3	b _ r _ _	3	_____
4	h _ us _	4	_____
5	b _ _ _ m	5	_____
6	p _ _ y	6	_____
7	s _ m _	7	_____
8	st _ _ m	8	_____
9	e y _	9	_____
10	h _ _ d	10	_____

Second half

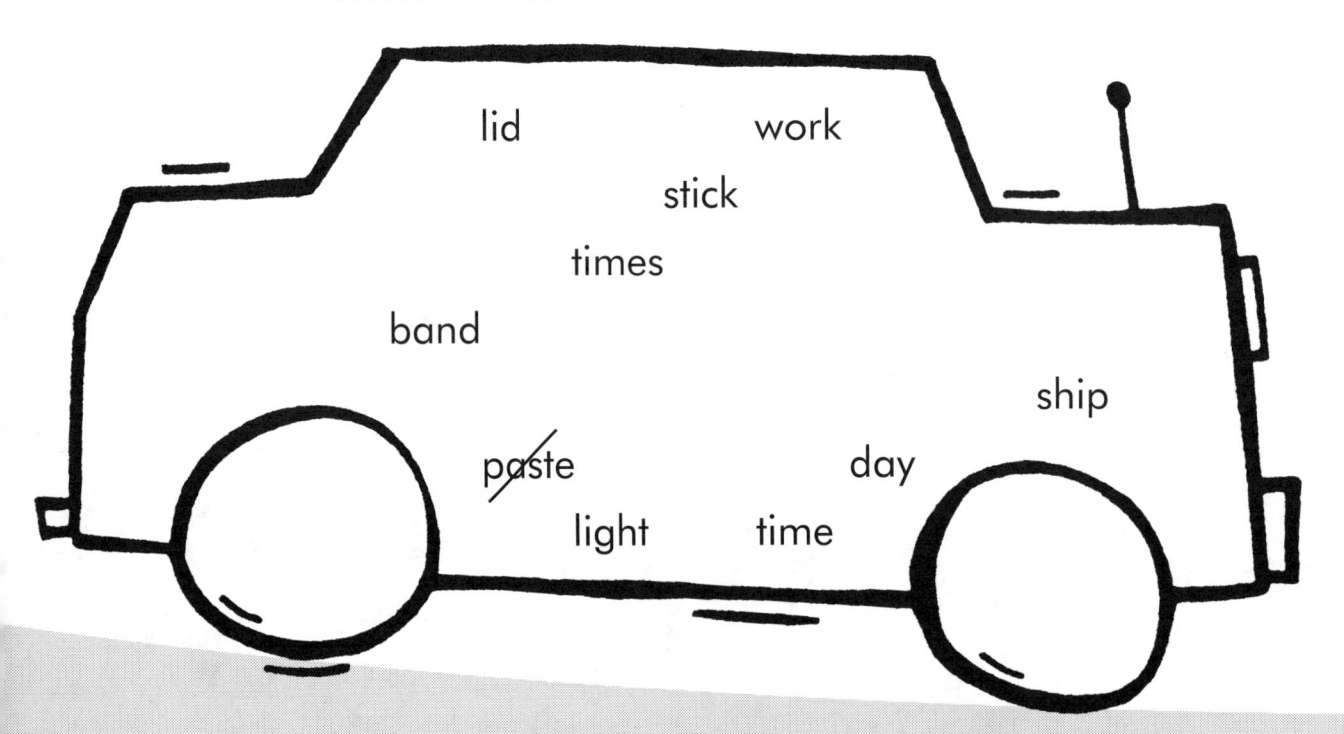

lid, work, stick, times, band, ship, ~~paste~~, day, light, time

98 ©N.Cahill & M.Pratt, *Literacy Skills Through Rhyme and Rhythm*, Oxford University Press, 1996.

CAR ATTACK
Reproducible Skill Sheet 3 — **Crossword**

Name: _____

Four words from the poem can each be written twice in the crossword. Find them.

STORM CAME

Clouds came
Scudding and soaring,
Storm broke
Raving, rip roaring.

In the garden
Branches bobbing,
In the drainpipes
Water sobbing,
In the doorways
Cats hobnobbing.

Rain eased
Drifting and trailing,
Clouds flew by
Wisping and paling.

Anger spent
Storm went.

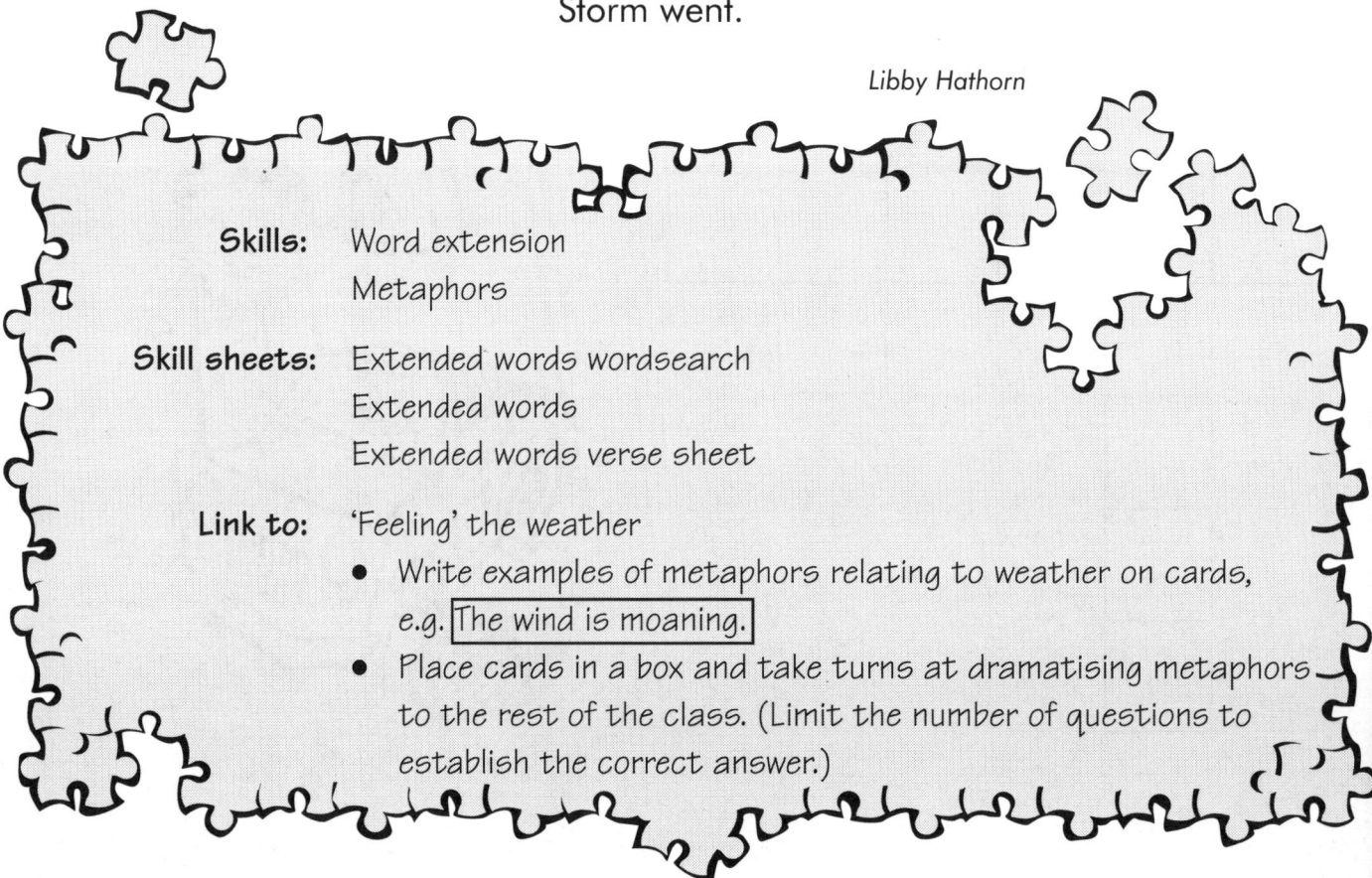

Libby Hathorn

Skills:	Word extension
	Metaphors
Skill sheets:	Extended words wordsearch
	Extended words
	Extended words verse sheet
Link to:	'Feeling' the weather

- Write examples of metaphors relating to weather on cards, e.g. The wind is moaning.
- Place cards in a box and take turns at dramatising metaphors to the rest of the class. (Limit the number of questions to establish the correct answer.)

STORM CAME

ORAL STAGE

- Recite the poem to the class.
- Recite the poem to the class again, this time clapping the main beat. Claps increase in speed and volume up to 'hobnobbing', then decrease to 'went'.
- Repeat as described above, with the children joining in.

Discussion: Storms—frightening or fun?

- Divide the class into two groups.

    Group 1 recites the poem while Group 2 chants the word 'storm' to the main beat.

- Ask questions at appropriate levels:

    1 What were the branches doing?

    2 Where were the cats?

    3 Why did the poet say the water was sobbing?

    4 How do you know the storm's anger was 'spent'?

    5 How do you feel when your anger is spent?

    6 What is meant when we refer to storms in our lives?

- Recite the poem together with the class.

    Children stand, arms raised, swaying to the main beat as they recite.

STORM CAME

WRITTEN STAGE

Visual presentation: Teacher/child uses a pointer and recites the poem, substituting or omitting words and/or consonants. Nominate a child to isolate and correct words.

Base Level

- Copy and distribute the Extended Words Wordsearch sheet (page 103).

    Ask the children to find the words. They colour all the base words red, and all the extended words yellow.

    Children write six of the extended words in sentences.

    Children illustrate the poem. They add labels to indicate the 'branches bobbing', 'cats hobnobbing', 'water sobbing'.

Middle Level

- Copy and distribute the Extended Words sheet (page 104).

    Children write over each base word and write the extension in the correct column.

    Children rewrite the poem, replacing all the extended words in verses 1 and 3.

    Ask them to draw a storm scene, attributing human qualities to some of the objects in their picture. Label them (e.g. flowers screaming).

Advanced Level

- Continue the 'storm' discussion.
- Read the poem and discuss the use of metaphors.

    Ask the children to imagine a storm in their lives—it could be emotional or physical. Then children write a story including some metaphors.

- Copy and distribute the Extended Word Verse sheet (page 105).

    Under each verse title children write a different storm verse within the shape. Use some extended words.

    Children create an acrostic using a 'storm' word.

STORM CAME
Reproducible Skill Sheet 1— Extended words

Name: _____

Word Search

1 Find all the base words and colour them red.

2 Find all the extended words and colour them yellow.

Base words	Extended words
scud	scudding
soar	soaring
roar	roaring
drift	drifting
trail	trailing
wisp	wisping
bob	bobbing
sob	sobbing
hobnob	hobnobbing

a	t	w	o	a	r	f	i	s	u	b	h	n	h
k	d	i	b	r	o	l	k	c	d	o	o	m	o
w	i	s	p	i	a	s	c	u	d	b	b	s	b
i	v	o	t	n	r	w	w	d	r	b	n	o	n
r	o	a	r	i	n	g	i	d	i	i	o	b	o
p	t	r	a	i	l	i	s	i	f	n	b	b	b
s	o	b	i	h	j	l	p	n	t	g	n	i	b
u	d	r	i	f	t	o	i	g	i	p	b	n	i
m	t	r	a	i	l	i	n	g	n	p	o	g	n
e	s	o	a	r	i	n	g	t	g	r	b	l	g

©N.Cahill & M.Pratt, *Literacy Skills Through Rhyme and Rhythm*, Oxford University Press, 1996.

STORM CAME
Reproducible Skill Sheet 2 — Extended words

Name: _____

1. Extend each base word by adding the correct ending.
2. Write over the base word and write its extended word in the correct column.

	add 'ing'		drop 'e', add 'ing'		double the last letter, add 'ing'	
	scurry	scurrying	skate	skating	hit	hitting
love						
ride						
worry						
walk						
take						
sob						
rave						
roar						
hike						
read						
fish						
run						

Can you add more? Can you see a pattern?

STORM CAME
Reproducible Skill Sheet 3 — **Extended Word Verse**

Name: _____

1. Write a short verse under each title.
2. Use some extended words.
3. Try some metaphors.

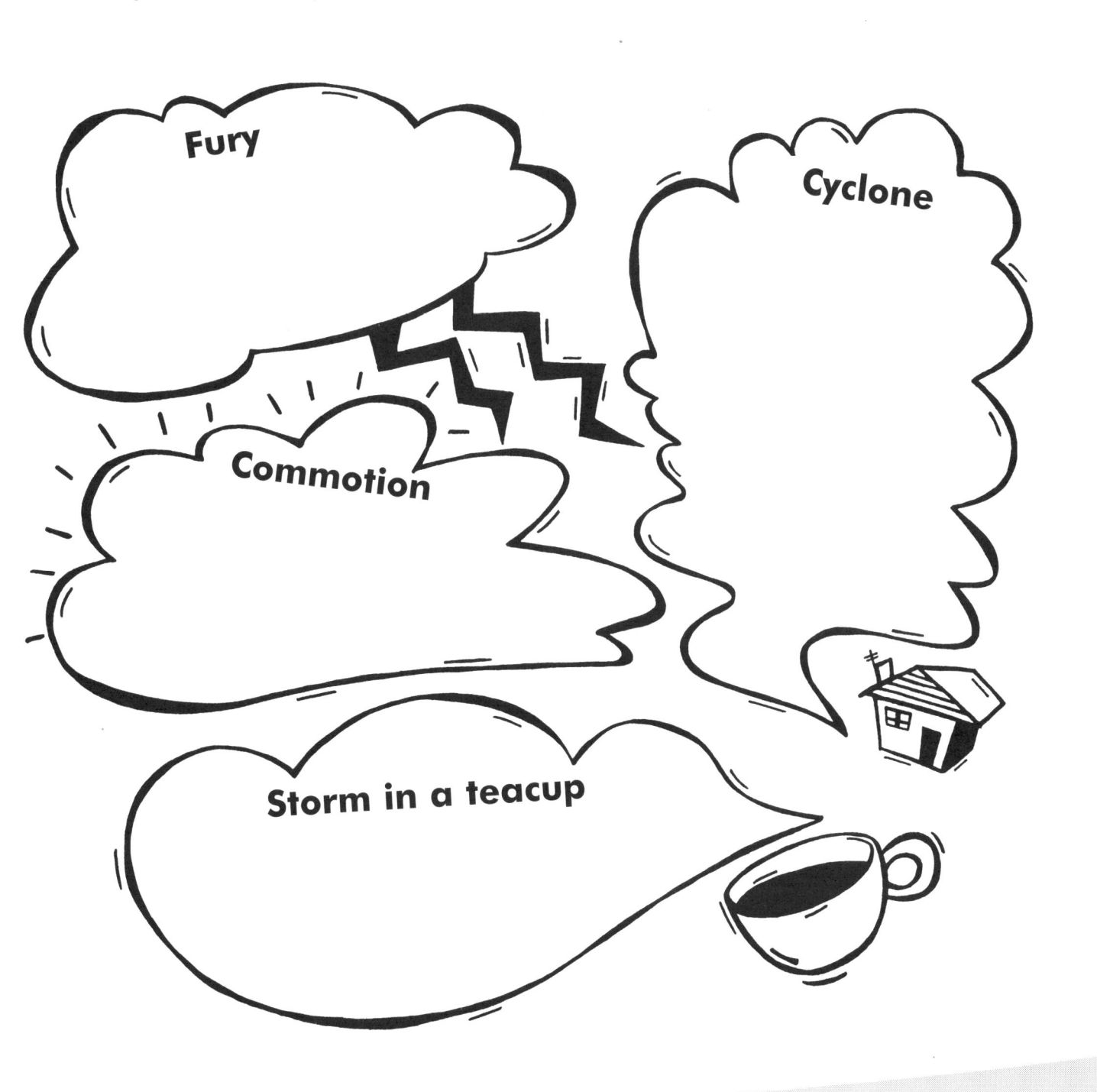

Fury

Cyclone

Commotion

Storm in a teacup

©N.Cahill & M.Pratt, *Literacy Skills Through Rhyme and Rhythm*, Oxford University Press, 1996.

Look what I can do

Date:

I made a comic strip . . . .

I put words from a poem in alphabetical order.

I made up a jigsaw . . . .

I found rhyming words. . . . .

I sorted words into families. . . . .

I wrote a poem . . . .

I made a booklet. . . . .

I made a wordsearch. . . . .

I made a thesaurus list. . . . .

I wrote an acrostic. . . . .

I made a shape poem . . . .

I wrote a poem on a wall chart. . . . .

I wrote a rhyming letter . . . .

What else can you do?

Poems I like

The Quangle Wangle's Hat
by Edward Lear
I liked it because _____
_____
_____
_____

_____
_____
I liked it because _____
_____
_____
_____

_____
_____
I liked it because _____
_____
_____
_____

_____
_____
I liked it because _____
_____
_____
_____

©N.Cahill & M.Pratt, *Literacy Skills Through Rhyme and Rhythm*, Oxford University Press, 1996.

Reproducible Record Sheet 3

My favourite poem